# SLAVISTIC PRINTINGS AND REPRINTINGS

edited by

C. H. VAN SCHOONEVELD

*Indiana University*

LXV

1966

MOUTON & CO.

THE HAGUE · PARIS

RUSSIAN COMEDY 1765-1823

# RUSSIAN COMEDY
## 1765-1823

*by*

### DAVID J. WELSH
*University of Michigan*

1966
## MOUTON & CO.
THE HAGUE · PARIS

Printed in The Netherlands by Mouton & Co., Printers, The Hague

Ce n'est pas mon dessein d'examiner maintenant
si tout cela pouvait être mieux, et si tous ceux
qui s'y sont divertis ont ri selon les règles.

Molière, *Les Fâcheux* (preface)

To. H. M.

# INTRODUCTION

This essay examines some representative comedies in the Russian repertoire from the theatrical season in St.-Petersburg (1764-1765) to the composition of Griboedov's *Gore ot uma* ("Woe from Wit", 1823). Particular reference will be made to the themes, characters and structure of the plays.

The genre was very copious; the *Dramatičeskij slovar'* (1787) lists some 300 plays produced in St.-Petersburg or Moscow before that date, of which most are comedies. The forty volumes of *Rossijskij teatr* (1786-1794) contain the texts of 71 comedies and 26 comic opera libretti, out of a total of 156 plays. These figures are remarkable, considering that the Russian theatre was not established until 1756, and Russian plays were not produced with any regularity until the 1764-1765 season.

Many of the eighteenth-century plays have been dismissed as worthless by critics ranging from Vjazemskij and Belinskij to critics of the Soviet period. But, as this essay seeks to demonstrate, the writers of the comedies considered here were talented and often highly-skilled craftsmen, who won the approval of their audiences. Such attributes meant much in the eighteenth century, particularly in Russia, where the theatre was so late in beginning. Besides, the work of these playwrights clearly reflects the taste and style of their age. They applied themselves to playwriting as a technique to be studied and mastered, not as a means of self-expression.

The playwrights' admiration for the French theatre cannot be overestimated. Yet their imitations, translations and adaptations of Molière and the rest consistently sought to produce plays with a recognisably Russian content. Because of these efforts, the plays make a significant contribution to the development of the Russian theatre, which would not exist in its present form without them. The plays of Ostrovskij, Čexov or Turgenev, for all their originality, belong to a national and traditional school of dramaturgy established by the craftsmen of the eighteenth century.

*Gore ot uma* opened a new era in the Russian theatre, though at the same time it marked the culmination of a tradition. The constituent elements of this tradition will be our concern in what follows.

Professor N. Gorodetzky (Liverpool University) guided and advised the writing from its inception. Professors John Mersereau and Horace W. Dewey (University of Michigan) made many invaluable suggestions. Publication was assisted by a grant from the Horace Rackham School of Graduate Studies, University of Michigan.

University of Michigan,                          DAVID J. WELSH
Ann Arbor

# CONTENTS

# TITLES OF THE PLAYS AND ABBREVIATIONS USED

*Alximist* (A. I. Klušin, 1793) – Alk.
*Bešenaja sem'ja* (I. A. Krylov, 1786) – Beš. sem.
*Bobyľ* (P. A. Plaviľšcikov, 1790) – Bobyľ
*Bogatonov* (M. N. Zagoskin, 1817) – Bog.
*Bogatonov v derevne* (M. N. Zagoskin, 1829) – Bog. v derevne
*Brigadir* (D. I. Fonvizin, 1764-9) – Brig.
*Čudaki* (Ja. B. Knjažnin, 1786/90?) – Čud.
*Derevenskij filozof* (M. N. Zagoskin, 1822) – Der. fil.
*Derevenskij prazdnik* (V. I. Majkov, 1777) – Der. praz.
*Dobryj malyj* (M. N. Zagoskin, 1819) – Dobryj mal.
*Fomuška babuškin vnuček* (P. A. Kropotov, 1785) – Fom.
*Gore ot uma* (A. S. Griboedov, 1823) – Gore.
*Jabeda* (V. V. Kapnist, 1793) – Jabeda.
*Kakadu* (A. A. Šaxovskoj, 1820) – Kakadu.
*Kofejnica* (I. A. Krylov, 1784) – Kof.
*Komedija protiv komedii* (M. N. Zagoskin, 1815) – Kom.
*Korion* (D. I. Fonvizin, 1765) – Korion.
*Lipeckie vody*, see *Urok koketkam*
*Modnaja lavka* (I. A. Krylov, 1805) – Mod. lav.
*Molodye suprugi* (A. S. Griboedov, 1815) – Mol. sup.
*Mužja ženixi svoix žen* (Ja. B. Knjažnin, 1784?) – Mužja.
*Nedorazumenie* (Catherine II, 1788) – Nedorazumenie.
*Nedorosľ* (D. I. Fonvizin, 1782) – Ned.
*Ne ljubo – ne slušaj* (A. A. Šaxovskoj, 1818) – Ne ljubo.
*Nerešiteľnyj* (N. I. Xmeľnickij, 1818) – Ner.
*Nesčastie ot karety* (Ja. B. Knjažnin, 1787?) – Nesčastie.
*Novyj Stern* (A. A. Šaxovskoj, 1805/7) – Nov. Stern
*Obmanščik* (Catherine II, 1785) – Obman.
*Oboľščennyj* (Catherine II, 1785) – Oboľ.
*Obraščennyj mizantrop* (A. O. Kop'ev, 1794) – Obr. miz.
*Opekun* (A. P. Sumarokov, 1765) – Opekun.
*O Vremja!* (Catherine II, 1772) – O Vremja.
*Perednjaja znatnogo bojarina* (Catherina II, 1772) – Pered.
*Pirog* (I. A. Krylov, 1802) – Pirog.
*Pritvornaja nevernosť* (A. S. Griboedov and others, 1818) – Prit.
*Pritvornaja sumasšedšaja* (Ya. B. Knjažnin, 1789) – Prit. sum.
*Prokazniki* (I. A. Krylov, 1788) – Prok.
*Pustodomy* (A. A. Šaxovskoj, 1819) – Pust.
*Rogonosec po voobraženiju* (A. P. Sumarokov, 1772) – Rog.
*Rozana i Ljubim* (N. P. Nikolev, 1776) – RiL.

*Šalosti vljublennyx* (N. I. Xmel'nickij, 1817) – Šalosti.
*Šaman sibirskij* (Catherine II, 1786) – Šaman.
*Sanktpeterburskii gostinnyi dvor* (M. Matinskii, 1779-81) – SPD.
*Sbitenščik* (Ja. B. Knjažnin, 1784) – Sbit.
*Ščepetil'nik* (V. I. Lukin, 1765) – Ščep.
*Skupoj* (Ja. B. Knjažnin, c.1782) – Skupoj.
*Sočinitel' v prixožei* (I. A. Krylov, 1786) – Soč.
*Svoja sem'ja* (A. A. Šaxovskoj, A. S. Griboedov and N. I. Xmel'nickij, 1817) –
   Svoja sem'ja.
*Traur* (Ja. B. Knjažnin, 1790) – Traur.
*Trumf* (I. A. Krylov, 1800) – Trumf.
*Urok dočkam* (I. A. Krylov, 1806) – Urok doč.
*Urok koketkam ili Lipeckie vody* (A. A. Šaxovskoj, 1815) – Urok.
*Urok xolostym* (M. N. Zagoskin, 1822) – Urok xol.
*G. Vestnikova s sem'eju* (Catherine II, 1772) – Vest.
*Vorčalkina* (Catherine II, 1772) – Vorč.
*Vozdušnye zamki* (N. I. Xmel'nickij, 1818) – Voz. zamki
*Xvastun* (Ja. B. Knjažnin, 1786) – Xvast.

The editions used are quoted in the bibliography.

# I.  THEMES

## The Russian Theatre and the Imperial Court

The Russian theatre of the eighteenth century was from the first closely associated with the Imperial Court, and reflected many of the interests, tastes and foibles of the ruling monarch.[1] The association began in 1701, when Peter the Great arranged for a company of German players under Kunst to be brought to St.-Petersburg. Kunst, and his successor Furst, were followed in 1729 by a small French company. An Italian troupe gave performances of *commedie dell'arte* and *intermezzi* at the Court of the Empress Anna in 1731, and again at intervals until 1739. Another German company, led by the celebrated Caroline Neuber, performed at the Winter Palace in April, 1740.

When Anna died, later that year, the pro-German element at Court was dismissed, and French cultural influences prevailed under her successor Elizabeth.

Five years later, the du Clos players performed at Elizabeth's Court during the celebrations of Princess Catherine's marriage to Peter Fedorovich: du Clos is believed to have included comedies by Molière, Nivelle de la Chaussée and Destouches in his company's repertoire. He stayed in St.-Petersburg for over a decade, but when Peter Fedorovich succeeded Elizabeth in December 1761, he gave vent to his detestation of everything French by dismissing the few remaining French actors.

This meant that when Catherine succeeded Peter Fedorovich to the Russian throne in June, 1762, the only theatrical companies at Court were Locatelli's *opera seria,* which went bankrupt later the same year, and a Russian company. The company had been established in 1756 by the Empress Elizabeth "for the presentation of tragedies and come-

[1] B. V. Varneke, "Teatr pri Ekaterine II", in *Istorija russkogo teatra*, ed. by V. V. Kallaš and N. E. Efros, I (Moscow, 1914), p. 155.

dies". Regular performances began in February, 1757.[2] At first, the company's director was the poet and dramatist A. P. Sumarokov, who resigned from the post in June, 1761, but continued to provide the company with much of its later repertoire.

During the early period of its existence, the Russian company at Court was led by the actor Volkov, and they performed tragedies of a classical kind by Sumarokov, Lomonosov and others, as well as adaptations and translations of comedies by Molière and his successors. The adaptations were also classical in tone: their characters personified general vices without special relevance to contemporary Russian conditions, and the settings were the "house which seems unattached to this world",[3] familiar from the French theatre of a hundred years before. Even the characters' names derived directly from seventeenth-century French comedies – Oront, Salmina, Fineta and the like.

Catherine soon found the productions of this company inadequate. Although a German princess by birth, Catherine's education as a girl had been French. At this period, the French stage still dominated the European theatre, as it had been doing since Molière. So, to indulge a fondness for the literature on which she had been brought up, and also as part of her attempts to introduce Western culture into Russia,[4] Catherine gave instructions within three weeks of her coronation in September, 1762, that a company of "good French players" be brought from Paris. The first company to arrive in St.-Petersburg in response to these instructions was the Clairval company, which Catherine generously subsidised during their stay in Russia. Their first performance at Court took place on September 26th, 1764, and initiated the winter theatrical season which lasted until the following February. During the season, the Russian company alternated with the Clairval company, presenting tragedies and comedies in Russian. However, Catherine's attitude can be judged by the way she attended only two of the Russian company's performances, but was present at nine performances by their French rivals.

Her lack of interest is understandable. Even as late as the 1760s, Russian literature and culture still had not "elaborated a set of values

---

[2]   R. A. Mooser, *L'Opera-comique français en Russie au XVIIIe siècle* (Monaco-Geneva, 1954) provides a lucid account of the Imperial theatres of the eighteenth century.
[3]   M. M. Meyer, *La convention dans le théâtre d'amour de Marivaux* (Sao Paulo, 1961), p. 55.
[4]   G. P. Gooch, *Catherine the Great and other studies* (London, 1954), p. 55.

and traditions which was uniquely its own . . . Russians, in their search for national identity, began to ask what the definitive features of the Russian way of life were, in which of them the national character most clearly revealed itself".[5] This uncertainty was reflected in the plays presented by the Russian company. Yet it was precisely this "search for national identity" as pursued in the theatre and in other kinds of literature too, which was to become a striking feature of Russian comedy during and after the 1764-1765 season.

An awareness of national identity was first shown in the Russian theatre by a group of writers and translators centred round I. P. Elagin. He was appointed "Director of Spectacles and Music at Court" in January, 1766, though he carried out several of the functions of the post earlier. Among the writers and translators for the stage whom Elagin encouraged were D. I. Fonvizin, V. I. Lukin and B. E. Elčaninov. They each provided one or more adaptations of French plays for the Russian company during the 1764-1765 season. Of the adaptations, Fonvizin's version of Gresset's *Sidney* (1745), which he called *Korion*, was the first attempt to adapt a French play in such a manner as to introduce aspects of contemporary Russian society by transposing the action to Russia.

Adaptations of foreign models to Russian conditions had already been practised in journalism by Elagin, in the 1750s, when he published a collection of translated essays. He said of them: "I did not translate literally, but omitted parts and added others, endeavouring to the transfer the foreign author to Russian manners."[6] This was the method used by Fonvizin in *Korion*, and the play may in turn have influenced Lukin, who defined the method more precisely and became its main spokesman in the theory of playwriting.

Lukin presented his arguments for a greater national awareness in the Russian theatre in prefaces to two plays he adapted from the French for the 1764-1765 season. He said:

Many spectators obtain no benefit from comedies based on foreign manners. When they see a comedy set in Paris or Versailles, the Russian audience think it is not they, but the foreigners, who are being laughed at. . . .

and:

[5] Hans Rogger, "The Russian national character; some eighteenth-century views", *Harvard Slavic Studies*, IV (1957), p. 17.
[6] A. O. Kruglyj, "I. P. Elagin. Biografičeskij očerk", *Ežegodnik imperatorskix teatrov*, IV, Supp. 2 (1893-4), p. 113.

... it has always seemed unnatural to me to hear foreign speeches in those
literary works which, by representing our manners, seek to correct not
only vices common to the whole world, but more particularly to our own
nation.[7]

Lukin did not suggest that Russian playwrights should compose original
comedies. Imitation was, after all, a highly respected literary mode in
the late eighteenth century. Besides, the Russian theatre had been in
existence for less than a decade. So Lukin's view was that the already
generally accepted method of adapting foreign models should continue,
provided that the resulting adaptations be transposed to Russian settings and manners, and deal with Russian society. Anything not rele-
vant to a Russian audience should be omitted.

These principles are illustrated in the eleven plays Lukin adapted
from the French repertoire between 1764 and 1773. His *Ščepetil'nik*
("The Trinker-vendor", 1765), itself an adaptation from Dodsley's
*Toy-Shop* (1732), introduced characters with Russianised names who
were satirised for displaying foibles of contemporary Russian society
such as Gallomania. Lukin also depicts two peasants, not present in
his French original, who use Russian dialect. He chose his title because
it was an "old-fashioned and traditional" Russian word. In general,
Lukin's adaptations of French comedies and sentimental dramas, in
which he consistently employed these methods, proved successful with
audiences, and helped form the taste of writers and the public.

However, Lukin's campaign for increased national awareness in the
Russian theatre had another, more personal aspect, in that it was at
least partly aimed against his rival, Sumarokov, who was the leading
representative of classicism. Lukin referred scornfully to Sumarokov's
plays and complained: "They are unsuccessfully taken from foreign
models, and thrust into our language almost by force." Sumarokov's
borrowings were not harmful in themselves to the development of the
Russian theatre, but his method was. Lukin went on to criticise the
"absurdity" of the names Sumarokov bestowed on his personages, and
the introduction of characters "unknown in Russian society", such as
a notary giving a couple in marriage. Sumarokov's "Harlequins" and
"Pasquins" meant nothing to Russian audiences.[8]

At first, Sumarokov's prestige in the theatre was so high that Lukin's

[7] B. N. Aseev, *Russkij dramatičeskij teatr XVII-XVIII vv.* (Moscow, 1958),
p. 211.
[8] P. A. Vjazemskij, *Polnoe sobranie sočinenij*, ed. by S. D. Šeremetev, V (St.-
Petersburg, 1880), p. 115.

attacks were dismissed as "mere disparagement of great works".[9] Hostility in the literary and theatrical world towards Lukin and his theories intensified when Catherine herself joined in the attacks against him, and mocked his style, orthography and opinions in her satirical journal. Derisive articles and malicious epigrams appeared by other writers, including the journalist N. I. Novikov, who published a parody of Lukin's theoretical prefaces in *Truten* ("The Drone", 1769).

Many of these attacks were inspired by personal antagonism rather than by dislike of Lukin's opinions for their own sake. Lukin was not on good terms with many of his contemporaries, whom he regarded as "dangerous rivals".[10] In the small world of St.-Petersburg society, writers still tended to consider their rivals as personal enemies; Fonvizin was able to express his contempt for Lukin's "low birth", and the playwright Ablesimov suspected Lukin of intriguing against the production of a comedy of his own.[11]

Yet, although Sumarokov and his comedies were the target of Lukin's attacks, Sumarokov was one of the first playwrights outside the Elagin group to be persuaded by Lukin's example. In the plays he wrote between 1768 and 1772, Sumarokov adopted several of the methods used and recommended by Lukin. His *Tri brata sovmestniki* ("The Three Rival Brothers", 1768) was an adaptation of Lafont's *les Trois frères rîvaux* (1713), into which Sumarokov introduced Slavonic names (Jaroslav, Svetoslav), transposed the setting to Moscow, and replaced the French aphorisms in his original by Russian proverbs.

Thus, despite the hostility generated by Lukin's campaign, the use of realistic detail in the form of Russian manners, settings and names rapidly became increasingly popular. Indeed, the predominance of the "comedy of manners" in Russian dramaturgy of the eighteenth century, discussed in more detail in Chapter II, owes much to Lukin's contribution to the "search for national identity". Nevertheless, Russian comedy continued to be dependent for several decades on the French theatre, although the Russian writers of 1765 and later turned for their characters, situations and plots to the older comedy of the seventeenth and early eighteenth centuries. Their models were the plays of Molière (died 1673), Regnard (died 1710), Destouches (died 1754) and other followers of Molière. They were less interested in the reforms and

[9] A. N. Pypin, *Istorija russkoj literatury*, 3rd ed., IV (St.-Petersburg, 1904), pp. 70-71.
[10] P. A. Vjazemskij, *op. cit.*, p. 27.
[11] I. M. Tupikov, "Satira na Ablesimova", *Ežegodnik imp. teatrov*, IV, supp. 2 (1893-4), p. 142.

developments in playwriting introduced by their contemporaries Diderot
or Beaumarchais into the theatres of Paris. What the Russian writers
admired and sought to emulate in their adaptations of the older French
comedies was the opportunity such plays afforded for satire and its
counterpart, moralising.

The Russian theatre felt the powerful flood of moralising which
overwhelmed eighteenth-century Europe. One of the primary functions
of the theatre was generally taken to be that of furnishing moral pre-
cepts to audiences. In England, Addison expressed the hope that the
theatre would "contribute its assistance to the advancement of morality
and the reformation of the age" (*Spectator*, no. 446, 1712). Destouches
followed suit when he said in the preface to his comedy *le Glorieux*
(1732): "I have always considered a comedy imperfect and even dangerous, if the author does not set out to correct manners ... and to
put virtue in such a light as to attract public esteem and respect."

Russian writers were in complete agreement with these views;
Lomonosov declared in his *Ritorika* (1748) that the theatre should
serve a social purpose. Sumarokov echoed Boileau's couplet: "Comedy
teaches us to laugh without spite ... It knows how to instruct and
how to cure", and added: "The attribute of comedy is to correct manners ... To amuse and cure is her direct rule." [12] Nearly twenty years
later, Lukin declared that, when translating plays into Russian, "It is
more important to correct manners than to display the beauties and
power of the foreign author." [13] In 1774, Novikov appealed in his
journal for plays containing "more moral lessons and examples".
Krylov (1792) called the stage a "tribute for castigating moral and
social vices", and this view was held by writers of the *Vol'noe
obščestvo ljubitelej slovesnosti* in the 1800s.[14]

### Moralising and Satire

The writers were also agreed that the most effective means of correcting faults and vices in society, and of instigating virtue was satire.
The mode flourished in eighteenth-century Europe, where writers regarded satire as a particularly rewarding method of attacking moral

---

[12]   D. M. Lang, "Boileau and Sumarokov; the manifesto of Russian classicism",
*Modern language Review*, 43 (1948), p. 504.
[13]   B. N. Aseev, *op. cit.*, p. 211.
[14]   I. A. Krjažimskaja, "Iz istorii russkoj teatral'noj kritiki konca XVIII – načala
XIX veka", in Akademija nauk S.S.S.R., *XVIII vek; sbornik statej.* IV (Moscow,
1959), p. 208.

and social faults because it was urbane, telling and at the same time diverting. They never forgot that moralising is all the more effective if practised according to the Horatian principle of "chastising while smiling".

Satire on the stage was directed against those aspects of their own society, of which the satirist-playwright disapproved. He set himself up as a judge, and would therefore propose certain standards of conduct while condemning others. Such is the nature of satire, however, that its practitioners are always more interested in the condemnatory aspect of the mode and are hence more successful in it. The Russian writers of satirical comedy were no exception, and although we may not find their "positive" moralising very rewarding, the satirical attacks still retain interest.[15]

Three satirical trends rapidly emerged in Russian comedy after 1765. Of these, two reflected the satire of the French stage: personal satire, or lampoons attacking specific and recognisable individuals, and more general satire aimed against vices, faults or foibles common to all mankind, such as hypocrisy, bigotry, superstition or affectation. The third trend, which soon overshadowed them, focussed upon satirical attacks against social, economic or political abuses which the playwrights regarded as characteristically Russian.[16] The trends were not mutually exclusive: recognisable individuals might be derided as representative of a general vice or folly, or vices common to all mankind might be satirised in a recognisably Russian setting.

## II

### Satire on Individuals

Personal satire attacking enemies is found in the comedies of classical antiquity (Plautus, Terence), and was a theatrical commonplace in the theatres of Western Europe during the eighteenth century and earlier. Keys identifying the originals of characters in Molière's plays had been circulated in Paris in the 1650s,[17] while the contemporary success of Etherege's *The Man of Mode* (1676) in London was attributed to

---

[15]  Quoted in I. A. Krjažimskaja, *op. cit.*, p. 206.
[16]  *Ibid.*, pp. 215-8.
[17]  Leon Levrault, *La comédie – évolution du genre*, 11th ed. (Paris, 1900), p. 55.

"the zeal with which everyone set out to seek the originals of its comic people".[18] Samuel Foote, the actor-manager, threatened in a celebrated incident reported by Boswell to "imitate Dr. Johnson on the stage" in 1775, and comedies deriding individual philosophers and their supporters were produced in Paris from 1750 until the Revolution.[19] In Russian comedy the device became so familiar that it merited technical names of its own, and comedies were said to be written "on an individual" ("na lico" or "na ličnost' "), and writers aimed to "introduce an original" ("vvesti podlinnik").

Lukin gave three reasons in 1765 why Russian playwrights wrote comedies: "the desire for fame, the need to make money and the wish to satisfy the envy, malice and spite which the writers feel personally against certain individuals".[20] These ironical comments were aimed, like Lukin's campaign for "narodnost' " in the theatre, against his rival Sumarokov, who is known to have used the device in a number of comedies. These included *Jadovityj* ("The Ill-natured Man", 1768), in which Sumarokov caricatured the journalist and novelist F. A. Emin as the malicious and boastful Gerostrat. This comedy was itself a response to Emin's *Učenaya šaika* ("The Band of Pedants", 1768) in which Sumarokov had been ridiculed as the foolish pedant Petroks and accused of plagiarism – a charge his rivals frequently levelled against Sumarokov. Other characters in Emin's one-act comedy have also been tentatively identified with contemporary individuals.[21] Sumarokov caricatured his own brother-in-law Buturlin, with whom he was involved in a law-suit; this was in the comedy *Lixojmec* ("The Usurer", 1768), and the caricature was so blatant that "even Buturlin noticed".[22] Lukin used the device: the poet Samoxvalov in his *Ščepetil'nik*, who complains that "no one here recognises the qualities of my works", informs the toy-shop vendor that "I know no books in Russian worth praising" and promises to write him a "panegyric epistle", is believed to be a portrait of Sumarokov, notorious for his hostility towards other contemporary poets and celebrated for his ability to compose panegyric

---

[18] John Palmer, *The comedy of manners* (London, 1913), p. 81.
[19] I. Ivanov, *Političeskaja rol' francuzskago teatra v svjazi s filosofiej XVIII-ago veka* (Moscow, 1895), pp. 358-88.
[20] P. N. Berkov, *Aleksandr Petrovič Sumarokov 1717-1777* (Leningrad, 1949), p. 57.
[21] I. Z. Serman, "Komedija F. Emina 'Učenaja šajka' ", in Akademija nauk S.S.S.R., *XVIII vek; sbornik statej*, III (1958), pp. 211-216.
[22] P. Rulin, "Elementy zlobodnevnosti v komedijax A. P. Sumarokova", *Slavia*, IV (1925-6), p. 728.

verses. Two characters in Lukin's sentimental comedy *Mot liubov'ju ispravlennyj* ("The Prodigal Converted by Love", 1765) were portraits "na lico" of individuals whom the audience recognised because the actors playing the parts "imitated the mannerisms, way of speaking and dress of the originals".[23]

Fonvizin's contemporaries were so accustomed to characters in plays being portraits "na lico" that a critic suggested his *Brigadir* in the play with this title (1768/9) was "drawn from an original", and declared that the audience recognised their own good or bad acquaintances in the characters of his *Nedorosl* ("The Minor", 1782).[24] Fonvizin admitted taking the *Brigadir's* wife from "an original – a Moscow acquaintance".[25]

The popularity of satire "na lico" in comedies of the late 1760s caused Catherine to formulate some views of her own on the device. As the population of St.-Petersburg was only a little over 150,000 people (1763), and the "society" from which theatre audiences were drawn was proportionally small, individuals portrayed in comedies were easily recognisable. Catherine could not approve of this. In her view, satire should be directed against general vices afflicting mankind as a whole, not against individuals. She therefore urged writers to exercise "philanthropy" since "it is impossible to find perfect human beings". To propagate this and other views which she held on the theatre and its moralising function, Catherine caused the journal *Vsjakaja vsjačina* ("Omnium gatherum") to be published from January, 1769. The editor was G. V. Kozickij, though the views were known to be those of the Empress.

Catherine was still anxious to acquire the reputation of an enlightened, even liberal monarch. For this purpose, she let it be known that the publication of other satirical journals, expressing other views, would be permitted. In this way she hoped further to propagate the ideas in her own journal through the medium of a literary polemic, one of the favourite occupations of eighteenth-century writers. Almost at once a number of other journals began appearing in St.-Petersburg and Moscow. Of these, the longest-lasting and most outspoken was Novikov's *Truten,* in which he voiced opinions on satire directly contradictory to those held by Catherine. In his view, only satire "na lico" was effective in correcting the vices and faults of society, and Catherine's

---

[23] A. Afanas'jev, *Russkie kritičeskie žurnaly* (Moscow, 1859), p. 93.
[24] K. V. Pigarev, *Tvorčestvo Fonvizina* (Moscow, 1954), p. 180.
[25] P. A. Vjazemskij, *op. cit.*

statements were thus "in defence of thieves and bribe-takers", not "philanthropic", but "vice-loving". Nor was Novikov the only writer to hold this opinion. He was supported by writers such as Ablesimov, who declared that "general satire mocking general vices is unnecessary", and favoured "personal satire based on actual individuals and current events". F. A. Emin too claimed in his journal *Adskaja počta* ("The Infernal Post", 1769) that satire "na lico" could not but help in correcting specific faults in Russian society.

Faced with this adverse critical opinion, Catherine revealed an aspect of her character which was to come to the forefront later in her reign; she closed down the journals which opposed her views. Nevertheless, comedy "na lico" persisted throughout her reign, and as late as 1793 Catherine herself was caricatured in two satirical comedies. These were *Smex i gore* ("Mirth and Woe") and *Alximist* ("The Alchemist"), both by A. I. Klušin. He was at this time an associate of I. A. Krylov, himself celebrated for his comedies "na lico" of the 1780s. In *Smex i gore* one of the central figures is a self-important, depraved, elderly woman greedy for power and attempting to buy love for money. Krylov drew particular attention to this creature when he reviewed the play, though he did not go as far as to state that Klušin's Mrs. Vzdorova was a portrait.

Klušin depicted another elderly woman in *Alximist*; here, Mrs. Vetroxrasova complains to the alchemist that her health has been "destroyed by love" and seeks to procure some of the alchemist's elixir. At this time Catherine was 64, and had just replaced her 25-year old favourite Zubov by his younger brother.[26] Catherine's very natural dislike of being ridiculed on the stage had already been illustrated by the incident which occurred during a performance at Court of Boissy's *Le Médecin par occasion*. A character in this play protested: "That a woman of thirty be in love – very well! But a woman of sixty – that is intolerable!" Although Catherine was still under fifty at the time, she left the theatre and the performance was hurriedly abandoned.[27]

Krylov was accused of malicious portrayals of his enemies in stage plays. He summarised one of the difficulties of writing satirical comedy when he advised writers in 1789: "Take care above all things not to attack vices, because a comedy written against any vice is regarded

[26]   P. N. Berkov, *Russkaja komedija i komičeskaja opera XVIII v.* (Moscow-Leningrad, 1950), p. 54.
[27]   R. A. Mooser, *L'opéra-comique français en Russie au XVIIIe siècle* (Monaco-Geneva, 1954), pp. 58-9.

as an attack upon an individual." [28] This comment illustrates the way in which the device was gradually expanding its scope: from attacking individual enemies, writers were coming to focus these attacks on individuals who – in their view – represented a vice or foible in contemporary society. Catherine employed this variation on the device in her comedies written after 1785, which are attacks on freemasonry. For one of her victims she chose the Italian charlatan Cagliostro, who had been well received in St.-Petersburg during one of his European tours in 1779. He appears as the self-styled mystics Kalifalkžerston and Amban Lej in Catherine's 5-act comedies *Obmanščik* ("The Cheat", 1785) and *Šaman sibirskij* ("The Siberian Magician", 1786) respectively. Both these personages deceive and rob honest but simple-minded Russians. The "mystic" Barmotin who tricks the foolish Radotov in Catherine's *Obol'ščennyj* ("The Deluded", 1785) into believing he has supernatural powers, and who introduces Radotov to "cabbalistic mysteries" was recognised by the audience as S. I. Mamalej, a Moscow devotee of freemasonry and mysticism who was also a friend of the satirical journalist Novikov.[29] All three of these comedies may also be taken as satirical attacks on Novikov himself, and on his attachment to freemasonry. Catherine's disapproval of freemasonry and its related sects of Rosicrucianism and Theosophism derived from their association in her mind with dangerous foreign influence, political opposition and subversion of both State and Church. In addition, Novikov represented liberal and enlightened ideas, and was for these reasons long the object of the Empress' displeasure, which culminated in his interrogation by State and later Church authorities between December 1785 and April 1786. Significantly, none of these comedies by Catherine was performed in Moscow, nor did the Moscow newspapers refer to them. Novikov had moved his printing-works there in 1779, and the city had become a centre of enlightenment and opposition to the Imperial court at St.-Petersburg. In fact, Catherine only visited Moscow three times during her reign – a period of thirty years. Thus, in all three plays the personal attacks – whether aimed against Cagliostro, Gamalej or Novikov – were little more than screens for Catherine's dislike of their dangerous activities. In this respect, the plays illustrate the growing tendency in the Russian theatre for comedies "na lico" to extend their scope and attack more general targets.

The tendency is also seen at work in plays attacking bad poets and

[28]  I. A. Krylov, *Sočinenija v dvux tomax*, I (Moscow, 1956), p. 294.
[29]  M. N. Longinov, *Novikov i moskovskie Martinisty* (Moscow, 1867), p. 112.

hack writers. At first, such attacks had been directed against the literary rivals and enemies of the playwrights. Personal enmity alone had prompted Sumarokov to compose his comedies "na lico" in the 1750s and 1760s: but Nikolev, while caricaturing Sumarokov as an individual in *Samoljubivyj stixotvorec* ("The Self-Satisfied Versifier", 1775) had extended his satire to attack all the bad poets of the period – for this was a time when the writing of verses was fashionable and might even prove a way to social advancement. Krylov castigated the species in his *Sočinitel' v prixozhei* ("The Author in the Vestibule", 1786) in his portrait of the plagiarist Rifmoxvat. His next comedy, however, appears to have been aimed specifically at Ja. B. Knjažnin, a supporter of Sumarokov and Krylov's literary rival. This was *Prokazniki* ("The Bombastics", 1787), one of the coarsest plays of this period, in which Krylov accuses his central figure, the poet Rifmokrad, of plagiarism and his wife Taratora of cuckolding her husband with Dr. Lancetin, a friend of the family. To ensure that his audience recognised the portrait, Krylov included in the play a malicious reference to the incident in which Knjažnin was reduced to the ranks for embezzling money (II, 3). Taratora is depicted as a foolish poetess, and in fact Knjažnin's wife was herself a poetess, and the daughter of A. P. Sumarokov. Dr. Lancetin in the comedy, who is clearly Taratora's lover, represents a certain Dr. Vien, suspected of cuckolding Knjažnin. When Krylov delivered his play to the Imperial theatre, Knjažnin – warned in advance – made certain it was not accepted, even though Krylov wrote a letter to Knjažnin protesting it contained no portraits "na lico". The play was not performed until 1793, after Knjažnin's death.[30]

Comedies "na lico" began to be increasingly used to attack rival literary groups. The "sentimental" writers were particularly vulnerable to "coterie gibes and informed allusions".[31] To make the satire still more pointed, parody was often used. Prijat's fondness for pastorals and eclogues (*Čudaki*, 1786/1790) holds up these genres to ridicule. Krylov's *Pirog* ("The Pie", 1802) introduces a sentimental lady whose exclamations of rapture at the "beauties of Nature" echo the affected diction of heroines in novels by Karamzin and his admirers. In 1804, A. A. Šaxovskoj echoed Krylov's attack on sentimental writers in *Kovarnyj* ("The Wily One") by presenting an Italian villain, Montoni,

---

[30]   I. A. Krylov, *Polnoe sobranie sočinenij*, ed. by V. V. Kallaš, I (St.-Petersburg, 1904), pp. 258-62.
[31]   Bertha Malnick, "The theory and practice of Russian drama in the early 19th century", *Slavonic and East European Review*, 34 (1955), p. 12.

who rhapsodises over "Nature in her manifold aspects", in order to ingratiate himself into the heroine's good books. The play also contains parodies of the "tirades" in sentimental drama by Kotzebue, and his imitators, popular on the Russian stage just then. Princess Kermskaja in the play rails at length against the "depravity of the world" in a manner familiar from those dramas. The absurd Pronskij of Šaxovskoj's *Novyj Stern* ("The new Sterne", 1805) declares he is too delicate for military service and falls in love with a peasant girl Malan'ja, whom he calls Melanie. This situation – a gentleman in love with a peasant girl – echoes the same situation popular in "sentimental" fiction such as Izmajlov's *Rostovskoe ozero* ("The Lake of Rostov", 1795) and Il'in's sentimental drama *Liza, ili Toržestvo blagodarnosti* ("Liza, or The Triumph of Gratitude", 1803). That Šaxovskoj's comedy was at least partly aimed at Izmajlov is suggested by certain textual analogies between *Novyj Stern* and a book by Izmajlov.[32]

The attacks launched by Karamzin's followers and admirers against Šaxovskoj's most celebrated comedy *Urok koketkam, ili Lipetskie vody* ("A Lesson for Coquettes, or Lipets Spa", 1815) were mainly inspired by the "personal nature of the satire which is directly aimed at specific individuals".[33] These individuals included the poet V. A. Žukovskij, ridiculed in the play as the sentimental ballad-monger Fialkin. Although this personage has only a subsidiary part in the intrigue of *Urok koketkam,* his role was deliberately brought into the foreground when the play was produced in Moscow. When it was given in St.-Petersburg, where Žukovskij was in attendance at court, the part was omitted.[34]

Šaxovskoj emphasized his satire by the use of parody: Fialkin's ballad, which he sings to the accompaniment of a guitar (II, 6) is a parody of Žukovskij's ballad *Ljudmila.* Fialkin's excessive fondness for the word "milyj" echoes Žukovskij's own frequent use of the word in his poetry.

Žukovskij was not the only individual caricatured in *Urok koketkam.* The malicious villain of the play Ol'gin was recognised as a portrait of S. S. Ugarov, described by a contemporary as "a gossip and intriguer,

---

[32] A. A. Šaxovskoj, *Komedii-stixotvorenija*, ed. by A. A. Gozenpud (Leningrad, 1961), p. 13.
[33] A. A. Šaxovskoj, *op. cit.*, p. 33.
[34] A. A. Šaxovskoj, *op. cit.*, p. 38. Žukovskij was present at a reading of the play at Šaxovskoj's house, and F. F. Vigel, who was present, said: "One can understand the indignation of Žukovskij's friends", cf. N. L. Brodskij, *Literaturnye salony i kružki* (Moscow-Leningrad, 1930), p. 49.

an admirer of foreign fashions, who has spent a long period abroad and is anxious to make himself a career in society at any price". The character named Ugarov in the play, an elderly rake, has several traits of V. L. Puškin, who is said to have been "on the verge of convulsions" during the first performance.

The controversy aroused by these satirical attacks on individuals was so fierce that it obscured Šaxovskoj's real target. The satire "na lico" in *Urok koketkam* was merely incidental to the main theme – satire against the attitude towards their homeland and society of the fashionable "umniki" such as Ol'gin. Instead of paying attention to this broader satirical topic, audiences and critics fastened immediately on the originals portrayed in a play. Šaxovskoj's supporter M. N. Zagoskin perceived this tendency when he commented on the device in his *Komedija protiv komedii* ("A Comedy against Comedies", 1815):

Personalities! This is the constant and most unjustified charge made against writers of comedy. A comedy ought to be a mirror in which every person can see his own likeness, but should not recognise himself. In writing a comedy, an author mocks vices – so it is not surprising that in giving to his personages characters which accord with the design of the piece and with the manners of his contemporaries he may – in the most innocent manner – make himself a circle of enemies. (II, 1)

This protest, uttered in the play by the hack writer Erastov, is of course disingenuous. Whatever its main purpose, the satirical comedy was and continued to be a satisfactory weapon for ridiculing a personal rival, and audiences then as now relished a recognisable caricature. Moreover, fifty years of tradition had led them to expect portraits "na lico" in comedy. So the habit of introducing and seeking originals in satirical comedy persisted on the Russian stage, and a decade later admirers of Griboedov's *Gore ot uma* ("Woe From Wit", 1823) continued to seek originals for its characters. Although Griboedov completed his play in 1823, it was not performed until 1831, and not published until 1833; however, despite these delays caused by official censorship, the play circulated in a large number of manuscript copies and was widely read.

Puškin joined in the identification of characters in *Gore ot uma*, when he reported: "They tell me he (Griboedov) has written a comedy 'na Čaadaeva'," [35] just as Šaxovskoj had written *Novyj Stern* "na Karamzina" and *Urok koketkam* "na Žukovskogo". After the first Moscow performance in 1831, the critic Nadeždin described the play

[35]   Letter to P. A. Vjazemskij, 1/8 December, 1823.

as "a living satirical picture, in which you involuntarily recognise originals".[36] Originals suggested later for Griboedov's rebellious and sarcastic hero Čackij included the poet V. K. Kjuxel'beker and Byron. Other characters in the comedy who have been "identified" with individuals known to Griboedov include the heroine Sofia and her father Famusov, believed to be portraits of a Mme. M. I. Rimskij-Korsakova, and her father. Members of Mme. Rimskij-Korsakova's household, where Griboedov was a visitor, were also said to have served as originals for characters in the play, "down to Petruška, the footman".[37]

Griboedov denied that his characters were portraits "na lico", and declared in a private letter: "I hate caricatures – you will not find one in my picture."[38] In view of this remark, the persistent efforts of Griboedov's admirers to identify his personages with real individuals bear witness to the frequency of satirical portraits "na lico" on the Russian stage. But, as Griboedov himself was well aware, the characters in *Gore ot uma* are drawn with a subtlety and skill which were beyond the talents of his predecessors and contemporaries.

## III

### *"General" Satire*

Satire of a more general and universal kind appeared on the stage parallel to satire "na lico". This general satire conformed closely to the satire of classical comedy as practised by Ben Jonson and, more particularly, Molière. Here satire was directed against vices, faults or foibles in human nature that were common to any civilised society, whether in London, Paris or St.-Petersburg. The central character was obsessed by his "humour" or vice, and the entire play was devised to illustrate this vice. Satire against such universal faults of character was associated exclusively with the *comédie de caractère*, and appears in Russian dramaturgy in the form of translations from Molière and his followers. The *comédie de caractère* is considered in more detail in chapter III, and in any case, satire against general vices of human nature never developed as copiously in the Russian theatre as satirical comedy "na lico" or satire relating to specifically Russian conditions.

[36]  A. M. Gordin, ed., *A. S. Griboedov v russkoj kritike* (Moscow, 1958), p. 62.
[37]  M. Geršenson, *Groboedovskaja Moskva*, 2nd ed. (Moscow, 1916), pp. 70-107.
[38]  Letter to P. A. Katenin, January 1825.

## Satire on Russian Conditions

The growing concern with ideas of "narodnost' " and "otechestvennost' " was primarily responsible for causing playwrights to concentrate their satire against conditions prevailing in their own society. The purpose of the satire remained unchanged – the correction of faults by ridicule – but the faults were now those abuses which the writers regarded as most harmful in contemporary Russian society.

As early as 1748 Sumarokov listed a number of abuses rampant in Russian society which seemed to him to require correction, and all these "vices" were to provide targets for satirists for the next fifty years and more. They were "bribery, the ignorance of judges, the affectation of dandies, the idleness of the nobility and the miserliness of the gentry".[39] Although conditions changed greatly during Catherine's reign – not always for the better – these faults continued to be satirised through the period described here, and in this respect Russian comedy again presents a parallel with the eighteenth-century French stage, in which "not one remarkable fact in social life escaped the attention of playwrights".[40] In Russia, however, Catherine exercised a more efficient and intense censorship than that to which the French stage was subjected. The texts of plays of this period which have survived are those which were approved by Catherine's censorship, and it is therefore only by implication that the playwright's satirical intention can be discerned. No doubt it was possible for actors to draw the attention of the audience by intonation or emphasis to an implication which the censorship had overlooked. In addition, the playwrights exercised a kind of auto-censorship, well knowing that a number of subjects and themes would, if treated satirically on the stage, render their work liable to confiscation and themselves to rebuke or punishment by the authorities.

## Censorship

Censorship of stage plays and all other kinds of literature intensified throughout Catherine's reign.[41] Although she sought to be a liberal and enlightened monarch when she ascended the throne in 1762, a "series

---

[39]   Aseev, *op. cit.*, p. 124.
[40]   Ivanov, *op. cit.*, p. 358.
[41]   A. M. Skabičevskij, *Očerki istorii russkoj cenzury* (St.-Petersburg, 1892), pp. 235-276 deals with this period.

of shocks – the savage rebellion of her own peasants, the collapse of
the French monarchy . . . transformed the Empress from an enlightened
to a frightened despot, from a patron to a censor, and finally to a
persecutor of writers".[42] She exercised her censorship in several ways;
by placing the management and financing of all the Court and later of
the public theatres in the hands of government officials, and also by
making her own appointments to administrative posts in the theatres.
Although she was more concerned, at least before the Pugačev peasant
rebellions of 1773-1774, with the literary theory of satire and its moral
purpose in correcting manners, yet she is known to have exercised
personal control over the plays presented at Court. Although Fonvizin
probably completed his *Brigadir* well before he gave Catherine a private
reading of the play in 1769, it was not performed at Court until 1772,
and not given in public until 1780.[43] Catherine may well have objected
to Fonvizin's ferocious mockery of ignorant provincial gentry, and to
his implied criticism of her own administration in the references to
bribery in law-courts and to usury (III, 6). Fonvizin also had difficulties
in obtaining permission for the production of his *Nedorosl'* ("The
Minor"), which, although completed by 1781, was not performed
until September 1782. Before this play could be produced in Moscow,
the local censor required the omission of a number of "dangerous
lines". No sooner had *Nedorosl'* been performed at the "Public Russian
Theatre" in Moscow, than Catherine took the precaution of placing
the theatre under State control. *Nedorosl'* was not produced at Court
until five years later, and although this was a shortened version, it
nevertheless brought upon itself the indignation of courtiers. They were
no doubt vexed by Starodum's moralising on the duties of enlightened
monarchs and gentry, implying they themselves were failing to carry
them out as Russian gentry should. Fonvizin's own "complete edition"
of his works was prohibited in 1788, as was a posthumous edition
planned in 1792.

Fonvizin was a remarkably outspoken critic of many aspects of
Catherine's reign, so that his difficulties with the censorship were to
be expected. In any case, official censorship was still widespread in
Western Europe, and its occurrence in Russia was by no means unusual at this period. Moreover, even such apparently innocuous trifles

[42]  R. W. Mathewson, "Russian literature and the West", *Slavic Review*, 21
(1962), p. 413.
[43]  G. Makogonenko, ed., *Russkie dramaturgi XVIII v.*, I (Moscow-Leningrad,
1959), p. 222: V. V. Kallaš and N. E. Efros, *Istorija russkogo teatra*, I (Moscow,
1914), p. 357 argue for 1763/4 as date of *Brigadir*'s composition.

as comic operas were also subjected to a close scrutiny by the censorship – both in France and Russia. The mildly satirical comments on the
"hard life" of peasants in Popov's *Anjuta* (1772) were toned down or
omitted for its production in the 1773 season. Nikolev's *Rozana i
Ljubim* (1776) was the "first serious attempt to depict the life of serfs",
but the libretto was "for long kept under lock and key" by the theatre
administration before it was finally produced in Moscow in 1778. A
copy survives in which a number of phrases have been "toned down".[44]
The intrigue of this piece deals with a landowner who kidnaps the
peasant girl Rozana and carries her off – captivated by her charms –
to his mansion. The ending is however "acceptable", in that the land-
owner repents his wicked deed and is forgiven by the serfs, whom he
promises to treat more kindly in future.

A number of other instances of imperial censorship occurred during
this period. After the Fall of the Bastille and execution of Louis XVI,
Catherine's censorship grew increasingly suspicious of writers. Indeed,
all other European governments took preventive action of one sort or
another after the French Revolution to guard against propagation of
revolutionary notions. In view of the prevailing atmosphere, it was all
the more courageous of the playwright and poet V. V. Kapnist to seek
permission for the production and publication of his satirical comedy
*Jabeda* ("Chicanery") in 1793. His attack on corrupt judges and law-
court officials in this play was as ferocious as Fonvizin's attacks on the
inhumane treatment of serfs and the deplorable results of faulty education in *Brigadir* and *Nedorosl'*.

Catherine refused permission, and Kapnist did not venture to approach the censorship department in St.-Petersburg until after her death.
The manuscript of *Jabeda* which Kapnist submitted for approval in
1797 has survived, and shows the cancellations which the censor required before allowing publication of the play in October, 1798. Four
months earlier, *Jabeda* had been produced with remarkable success in
St.-Petersburg, only to be withdrawn at the insistence of offiicals fear-
ful of seeing their own corruption exposed.

Tsar Paul shortly afterwards commanded a private performance of
the play for his own delectation, and is said to have sent a messenger
post-haste with an imperial pardon for the unfortunate playwright,
who had already been despatched to Siberia. But there is no evidence
that this agreeable incident took place, and the play was excluded from

---

[44]  Aseev, *op. cit.*, pp. 305-6.

the repertoire in September, 1798.[45] The revival of 1808 is discussed below.

I. A. Krylov, later celebrated for his fables, also encountered difficulties with the authorities in St.-Petersburg, although the precise nature of the difficulties remains obscure. In any case, none of his comedies or comic operas was produced in St.-Petersburg, and *Trumf* (1799), ostensibly a parody of classical tragedy, was only presented privately. The play depicts one of the conventional "enlightened monarchs" of Russian classical tragedy, who is portrayed as a cowardly egoist surrounded by sycophantic foreign courtiers. The situation must have been dangerously suggestive to a contemporary audience of conditions prevailing at Tsar Paul's court.

Although the censorship relaxed somewhat during the early years of the reign of Tsar Alexander, Kapnist's version of Molière's *Sgnarelle* (1806) met with disapproval for its "unseemly expressions" such as "cuckold" and the like.

The delay in performing and publishing Griboedov's *Gore ot uma*, mentioned above, was also due to problems of censorship. But Griboedov was so eager to have his comedy produced that, like many playwrights before and after him, he acted as his own censor, making alterations and omissions in the original version of the play before submitting it. Even so, the Moscow censor refused him permission, and when the play was finally published in 1833, after the playwright's death, it was "almost unrecognisable to a public which already knew the play in manuscript copies".[46]

Despite the constant pressure exerted by both State and Church throughout Catherine's reign and later, the Russian playwrights persisted in attacking a number of manifest social and other abuses of their time. They were not alone: many of their comedies echo or foreshadow similar attacks launched by the satirical journals which flourished intermittently after 1769. A. N. Radiščev's *Journey from Petersburg to Moscow* (1790) is another case in point. Radiščev castigated the institution of serfdom still more outspokenly than even Fonvizin had ventured to do in *Nedorosl'*. But it was easier, after all, to arrange for the publication of a book – clandestinely, under a pseudonym or anonymously – than to have a play produced in the theatre.

---

[45] V. V. Kapnist, *Sobranie sočinenij v dvux tomax*, ed. by D. S. Babkin, I (Moscow-Leningrad, 1960), p. 750.

[46] A. M. Skabičevskij, *op. cit.*, p. 276. "More than 40,000 manuscript copies" of *Gore ot uma* were circulated according to Boris Klejber, "Zagadki *Gorja ot uma*", *Scando-Slavica*, VIII (1961), p. 37.

## The Targets of Satire

All the same, a number of targets continued to be attacked on the stage. They range from more or less innocuous foibles such as the pursuit of titles or rank, snobbery in fashionable society, the conflict between older, Petrine traditions and the innovations of Catherine: the attitude of gentry towards their homeland, to government service or their serfs: to the vices and faults listed by Sumarokov, and extending as far as criticism of aspects of the State itself.

The gravity of the vices satirised tended to be in inverse proportion to the comic elements in the plays. This was natural enough, for serious social abuses having painful or disagreeable associations for an audience were not suited to satire. Contemporary and later critics frequently made this point: when Fonvizin attacked the consequences of faulty education or the inhumanity of provincial gentry to their serfs, and when Kapnist derided corruption in the law-courts, critics complained that the plays "lacked comedy".[47] Laughter in the theatre aroused by the characters in *Nedorosl'* changed into "troubled pondering" when the audience left the theatre.[48] As a result, writers of comedy concerned themselves most often with the more harmless foibles of society, with moralising and exhorting virtue.

Discussing this aspect of eighteenth-century comedy in an essay published in 1859, the critic N. A. Dobroljubov drew analogies between his own age and that of Catherine:

Hardly ever did the satirists of the eighteenth century penetrate to the main, essential evils. .... The nature of their accusations was private, cursory and superficial. .... Their satire against such abuses as bribe-taking by government officials gave the impression that the whole evil depended upon the personal tendencies of these officials.

He adds that the playwrights' attitude was "that of a doctor, telling his patient he ought to be healthy".[49]

Even Novikov, perhaps the most outspoken of the satirical journalists of Catherine's reign, was careful not to question in his writings

[47] Zagoskin is quoted by N. I. Mordovčenko, *Russkaja kritika pervoj četverti XIX veka* (Moscow, 1959), p. 238; Vjazemskij in his *Polnoe sobranie sočinenij*, V (St.-Petersburg, 1880), p. 135; Belinskij in his *Polnoe sobranie sočinenij*, VIII (Moscow, 1955), p. 119; Gogol' in his *Polnoe sobranie sočinenij*, IV (Moscow, 1953), p. 470.
[48] Quoted in A. A. Kaev, *Russkaja literatura*, 3rd ed., I (Moscow, 1958), p. 531.
[49] N. A. Dobroljubov, "Russkaja satira v veke Ekateriny II", in his *Sobranie sočinenij v trex tomax*, II (Moscow, 1952), pp. 317-8.

the overall structure of the existing order. This was the basic principle by which playwrights were continually guided too. They held fast to the assumption that Catherine's reign was "completely good, except for some vestiges left over from the past",[50] which Catherine herself condemned, and which were therefore eminently suitable targets for satirical attacks. As soon as Catherine issued a decree abolishing bribe-taking, playwrights and journalists felt at liberty to seize upon and exploit the topic – but they were always careful to insist that bribe-taking was "now" a "vestige of the past". This ingenious device was generally adopted as a safeguard whenever a serious abuse was attacked.

IV

*Pursuit of Rank*

Among the more innocuous foibles prevalent in Russian society which the playwrights delighted in castigating was the pursuit of rank and orders by lesser gentry or newly-rich merchants. As a theme for comedy this had already been handled by Molière and other French playwrights of the seventeenth century. But the topic had gained particular significance in Russia, for it reflected Catherine's notorious generosity in bestowing titles and wealth upon her favourites at Court.

Among newly-rich merchants ridiculed on the stage for their eagerness to acquire a title and the right to wear a sword which accompanied the title was Razmotaev, in Količev's *Dvorjanjuščejsja kupec* ("Merchant turned Gentleman", 1780). Razmotaev is tricked by the impoverished Graf Peresmešnikov into believing that the latter can assist him obtain a title. Razmotaev even visits the theatre to see Molière's *Le Bourgeois Gentilhomme* without suspecting that the satire is applicable to himself (act II). The sequel to this play was the anonymous *Peremena v nravax* ("A Change in Manners", 1789), in which the merchant Bogatonov is portrayed yearning for a title and accompanying sword. The sword as a symbol of gentry is also anxiously sought by Knjažnin's merchant Boldyrev in the comic opera *Sbitenščik* ("The Sbiten-seller", 1784).

Knjažnin suggests the attitude prevailing in Russian society towards the acquisition of rank by means of influence in his *Xvastun* ("The

[50] *Ibid.*, p. 350.

Braggart", 1786); in this play, the foolish Prostodum, a representative
of the provincial gentry, eagerly offers the braggart Verxolet money
when the latter claims he can obtain for him the rank of senator.
Verxolet's offer does not surprise Prostodum or any of the other characters, who take it for granted that the rank can be purchased for
money by anyone prepared to pay.

The character Bogatonov re-appears in two comedies on snobbery
by Zagoskin: his *Gospodin Bogatonov* ("Mr. Bogatonov", 1817) and
*Bogatonov v derevne* ("Bogatonov in the Country", 1820). In these
plays Zagoskin depicts Bogatonov's attempts to penetrate fashionable
society, in which he is tricked and held up to ridicule by other
characters. But Zagoskin's attitude towards his Bogatonov differs from
that of his predecessor, the anonymous author of *Peremena*, in that
Zagoskin's target is the fashionable society into which the hapless
Bogatonov wishes to enter. Zagoskin derides the fashionable coquettes
and "umniki", while his Bogatonov is a foolish old man more to be
pitied than blamed for his illusions about worldly society.

### Old and New Traditions

Another feature of Catherine's reign which playwrights treated satirically was the conflict between old and new traditions. But this topic
was one in which some caution was required before it could safely be
satirised on the stage, whereas the pursuit of titles and rank was merely
a vestige of the past. This conflict, an essential element in Russian
social life during the eighteenth century, had originated in the reforms
of Peter the Great. In the first two decades of the century, he attempted
to introduce western manners into what had hitherto been a highly
conservative society. The aristocracy and gentry saw these reforms as
threatening their own position and privileges. Attempts such as the
1762 decree freeing the gentry from obligatory military service had
been made to conciliate thcm, but the hostility persisted. Moscow was
at the same time the centre of the older Petrine traditions and of
European enlightenment, whereas St.-Petersburg was the seat of the
Imperial court and government departments representative of the new
traditions.

The conflict was thus closely connected with the monarchy itself,
which meant that satire attacking the traditions of the past might well
prove offensive to Catherine's family pride. As a foreign princess, she

felt the need during the first part of her reign to publicise her admiration and respect for her august predecessor, Peter the Great.[51] On the other hand, praise of the present in a satirical comedy would imply criticism of the past.

The way playwrights dealt with the conflict is best illustrated in comedies dealing with relations between parents and children. Catherine's own plays are ambiguous towards the theme. The early comedies satirise the conservative, older generation of Muscovites who "praise and love the past". They include Mrs. Xanžaxina in *O Vremja!* ("O Time!", 1772), and Mrs. Vestnikova in *Gospoža Vestnikova s sem'eju* ("Mrs. Vestnikova and her Family", 1772). Both these ladies are depicted, as their speaking names suggest, as hypocritical, malicious and discontented with the state of society. The querulous Mrs. Vorčalkina of *Imeniny gospoži Vorčalkinoj* ("The Namesday of Mrs. Vorchalkina", 1772) is said to "keep to old-fashioned ways" merely out of laziness and habit. She refuses to let the heroine of the play marry before an elder daughter is married off, "because I myself suffered in this way as a girl". She boasts of having married her own husband "without ever seeing him previously" (II, 6). Catherine is holding up to derision the system of arranged marriages which had survived in conservative society since pre-Petrine times.

Yet the younger generation in Catherine's plays, who might have been depicted as enlightened and rational in contrast to their parents, is equally ignorant, badly brought-up and discontented. Vorčalkina's elder daughter Olimpiada is indolent and vain, rises at eleven in the morning and spends "four hours a day at her toilette". The 15-year old heroine of *O Vremja!* has been taught "gramota" by the servant girl Mavra, but knows hardly any Russian and cannot even carry on a rational conversation.

Occasionally, playwrights show children in rebellion against their parents, though – like Catherine – they rarely take sides in the conflict. Ivan challenges his father, the Brigadir (who has called him a fool) and demands: "Do I owe you the slightest respect?" (*Brig.*, III, 1). But the Brigadir is as ignorant in his own way as Ivan. Sobrin's son Ivan, in Catherine's *Razstroennaja sem'ja* ("A Distracted Family", 1772), flaunts his father's orders not to leave the house without parental permission: he immediately falls into bad company, is cheated at cards, and brought home in disgrace from a disorderly house (IV, 8). The

[51] P. N. Berkov, *Satiričeskie žurnaly N. I. Novikova* (Moscow-Leningrad, 1951), p. 13.

heroine Ljubov in A. D. Kop'ev's *Obraščennyj mizantrop* ("A Misanthrope Converted", 1794) is reduced to tears by her parent's stupidity,
but Kop'ev clearly has little or no sympathy for her either.

The conflict was also illustrated in the relations between members
of the conservative and patriarchal society of Moscow, and the "petits-
maîtres" and Frenchified fops with their admiration for everything
foreign. But this aspect is closely associated with the emergence in
Russian society after 1815 of the fashionable "umniki", and will be
considered in more detail in that context.

# V

## Malpractices in the Administration

Malpractices in the administration, particularly the provincial law-
courts, had been the object of satire from the sixteenth century, expressed in popular sayings and verses. These malpractices were usually
manifested in the form of bribery, and they were fomented by the
chaotic state of legislation. The "Code of Laws" drawn up in 1649 by
Tsar Alexej Mikhailovich had been added to and amended so frequently that it was already out of date by 1700, when a commission
was appointed to revise and issue a new code. This attempt failed, as
did others. In the 1730s, the satirist Kantemir derided the conditions
of Russian law-making and the administration of justice, and the subject was also satirised by writers such as Pososkov and Prokopovič.
The confused state of the legislation encouraged the arbitrary inter-
pretation of laws in favour of a plaintiff able to bribe the judge, and
also encouraged a fondness for litigation.

Catherine's own relish for laying down the law persuaded her to
make several attempts to approve this state of affairs. As early as
1766 she sought to form a commission to draft a new legal code, but
this attempt failed, and the system continued as before. Yet when
Novikov ventured to publish articles condemning wide-spread bribery
in the law-courts, Catherine indignantly refuted the charge as "lies",
though she went as far as to admit that if sporadic cases might occur
in the provinces, they were nothing more that a "vestige of the past",
and were rapidly being amended. Writers dealing satirically with the
topic followed her example, and stated clearly that bribery was a thing
of the past. Fonvizin's Sovetnik in *Brigadir* admits he took bribes when

serving in a provincial law-court, but was "forced into retirement" by the 1762 decree aimed at abolishing the abuse. Dobroljubov in the same play declares that "*formerly* it was possible to expedite a judgment by bribing court officials", but "*nowadays* judges dare not accept bribes" (III, 6).

Another convenient and relatively safe way of satirising bribery in the law-courts was that used by Volkov in *Vospitanie* ("Education", 1773), where the judge's wife accepts money from litigators "so as to keep my husband's hands clean". Similarly, the court secretary in Verevkin's sentimental comedy *Tak i dolžno* ("How Things Ought to Be", 1773) accepts bribes on behalf of his master, the Palatine Bezčetnoj. Elsewhere in this play, the hero Doblestin accuses Bezčetnoj of unlawfully holding his aged parent in prison. Doblestin threatens to appeal to the Empress herself if the Palatine refuses to release the old man, implying that this abuse of the law would quickly be remedied if Catherine were aware of it.

Kapnist's *Jabeda*, which – as we have seen – caused its author such difficulties with the censorship in the 1790s, was the apotheosis of Russian satirical comedy attacking corruption in the law-courts. *Jabeda* is one of the most striking examples of the eighteenth-century comedies of which critics complained that "nothing in its action or characters is comic or diverting".[52] During four of the play's five acts, the corrupt provincial judge Krivosudov, his termagent wife Tekla, his court officials and servants are all depicted soliciting and accepting bribes from petitioners, getting drunk and falling asleep during court proceedings – until, in a denouement reminiscent of *Nedorosl'*, the crimes of Krivosudov come to the attention of a "higher authority", and he is dismissed. The same denouement was also used by Sokolov in his *Sudejskie imeniny* ("A Judge's Name-day", published in 1780, though written and set in the 1760s). Here the corrupt judge Xamkin's property is confiscated for usury, and he is arrested in the final scene.

The intrigue of Kapnist's *Jabeda* is as slight as the intrigue of most eighteenth-century comedies, for he, like his contemporaries in the theatre, was primarily concerned with the opportunities furnished by the plot for satirical treatment. Whenever possible, he insists that his portrayal of Krivosudov and his law-court were no longer true of Russian legislation. In the preface to *Jabeda*, he declared:

---

[52] V. N. Vsevolodskij-Gerngross, *Russkij teatr vtoroj poloviny XVIII veka* (Moscow, 1960), p. 273.

I must point out that in my comedy I have depicted members of a former
civil court, of which the composition and the powers have, as the result of
various faults, long since been altered by the Sovereign ... I hope impartial
readers will not accuse me of having held up to public ridicule the blame-
worthy activities of a court that has now ceased to exist ... No one feels
more than I do the respect due to any worthy servant of the Empire and
our homeland.[53]

The production of *Jabeda* which took place in 1808 emphasised that
the play was set "in the past". The officials played "Bank", "Picquet"
and "Rocambole", so that "some of the audience declared 'It was just
like that in the olden days'".[54]

We may doubt whether these transparent precautions deceived the
contemporary audience. The play was very successful indeed, both at
its first performances in 1798 and at its revivals in 1808 and 1812. In
1808 "even the boxes were all taken, which is rare at Russian productions", and the spectator who testified this added that "every word
bearing witness to an enormity of injustice, to chicanery and deceit was
applauded ... The celebrated chorus of tipsy officials, singing a song
which declares that 'hands are given to seize with' was encored several
times".[55]

These manifestations show that the audiences regarded the play
as typical of their own times, and Kapnist succeeded in suggesting
this when Fekla, the judge's wife, declares: "It is like this everywhere
– throughout Holy Russia ..." (IV, 4). The perfunctory way in which
the denouement is brought about also suggests that it was merely added
to satisfy the censor, as in the other comedies which use the same
device to bring their intrigues to a close.

The interest of *Jabeda* and its significance in the development of
the Russian comedy lie – like Fonvizin's *Nedorosl'* and Griboedov's
*Gore ot uma* – in the social aspect of the plays, which transcends the
artificialities of plot and characterisation, and the classical conventions
which occupy a large place in the structure of the plays.

The fate of *Jabeda* at the hands of the censors made it plain to
other writers that law-courts, bribery and corruption were not suited
to satirical treatment on the stage. From this time on, references to
these topics disappear, with the exception of Sudovščikov's *Neslyxan-
noe divo, ili čestnyj sekretar'* ("An Unheard-of Wonder, or The Honest

---

[53] V. V. Kapnist, *Sobranie sočinenij*, I (Moscow-Leningrad, 1960), p. 748.
[54] *Ibid.*, p. 748.
[55] *Ibid.*, p. 748.

Secretary", 1802), which introduces another judge named Krivosudov, no doubt derived from his original in *Jabeda*. Passing references of a satirical kind to bribery in the law-courts occured in Zagoskin's *Urok xolostym* ("A Lesson for Celibates", 1822), where the heroine explains that her father remained poor all his life "because he was a judge who never took bribes" (sc. 2). Mrs. Zvonkina, in this play, refers to a public prosecutor Caplin, who "lined his pockets" while pursuing his official occupation, but was discovered and sent to prison (sc. 8).

## VI

### *Serfdom*

As with other serious abuses of the time, playwrights had to approach serfdom and the peasantry with the utmost caution. Catherine's view of this matter during the early part of her reign were made clear in her decrees of 1765, which permitted land-owners to sentence their serfs to penal servitude ("katorga") and prohibited serfs from petitioning the Empress personally against ill-treatment by their owners. The attitude of the land-owners towards their serfs is clearly illustrated in the proceedings of the 1767 Comission on serf laws, during which members discussed whether or not they had the right to punish serfs, and how far these rights extended. The abolition of serfdom was not mentioned; at the most, proposals were made for establishing a "third estate" on Western lines, in addition to the gentry and peasantry. This class was to consist of "persons engaged in the arts, sciences, seafaring, commerce and handicrafts, and those who graduated from schools". But many of these people were absorbed into the Government service and thus attained the rank of gentry.[56]

The peasant rebellions led by Pugačev in 1773 and 1774 alarmed Catherine greatly. This fact in itself made the institution of serfdom a topic better not touched upon at all. In any case, it is doubtful whether any but the most enlightened and humanitarian people of the time even conceived of serfdom as an institution which might be abolished. To most Russian gentry, serfdom was part of the natural order of things.

Nevertheless, the serfs constituted an inescapable and indeed essential part of Russian society, and any writer attempting to depict Rus-

---

[56]   V. I. Pokrovskij, *Fonvizin – žizn' i tvorčestvo* (St.-Petersburg, 1903), p. 50.

sian manners on the stage could not ignore them entirely. So the play-wrights adopted various ingenious devices for depicting peasants in their comedies. Some, like Fonvizin, implied that inhumane land-owners were not worthy of being gentry; others, like Nikolev, suggested that the serfs were too ignorant and idle to fend for themselves, and would perish were it not for the benevolence of their owners; yet others, like Majkov, insisted on the paternal relationships supposed to exist between land-owners and their serfs.

Sumarokov had been one of the first playwrights to introduce serfs and the serf question into the theatre. He held high ideals of the duties of the aristocracy and gentry, and regarded them as playing a guiding role in society. In Sumarokov's view those land-owners who were cruel to their serfs were unworthy of belonging to the Russian gentry. His wealthy Mrs. Burda in *Vzdorščica* ("The Shrew", 1772) is an example of this species. Knjažnin clearly held the same views in his comic opera *Neščastie ot karety* ("Misfortune from a Carriage", 1772, performed 1779). The setting of this libretto is "the estate of Mr. Firjulin, not far from St.-Petersburg", and the action depicts the sufferings of two serfs, who are to be sold at the order of Mr. Firjulin, in order to purchase a French carriage for his wife. Both the Firjulins are afflicted with Gallomania, and are too grotesque to be considered as representative of Russian gentry. To be on the safe side, Knjažnin took the precaution of employing a frequently-used device to obtain a happy ending and to exculpate the Firjulins: they throw the blame for the sale of the two serfs upon their overseer, who is held responsibile for the entire in-cident. Krylov, too, makes the overseer guilty of cruelty to serfs in his comic opera *Kofejnica* ("The Fortune-teller", 1783). A still earlier in-stance of the device occurs in Fonvizin's *Korion* (1765): the hero's valet Andrej treats Korion's serfs in a brutal manner, though Korion himself is humane towards them. We need not speculate how far this sort of "tyranny through agent" was prevalent in eighteenth-century Russian society.

Fonvizin handled the topic of serfdom in a bold and outspoken manner in *Nedorosl'*. His cruel land-owner Mrs. Prostakova is more than a caricature, as the Firjulins were. She exemplifies the misuse of the arbitrary powers which gentry possessed over their serfs. Her in-dignant exclamation: "Is not a *dvorjanin* allowed to flog his servant if he wants to?" (V, 4), has been taken as the play's essential idea.[57]

---

[57] K. V. Pigarev, *Tvorčestvo Fonvizina* (Moscow, 1954), p. 155.

The play's denouement makes it clear that Mrs. Prostakova is unworthy of belonging to the Russian gentry: her estate is confiscated as a result of her inhumanity. Indeed, the play has been considered as a plea for more humanitarian treatment of serfs, though Fonvizin was equally anxious to castigate Prostakova's cruelty as a moral fault. Starodum emphasizes this when, in the final tableau, he points an accusing finger at her and exclaims: "We see here all the miserable consequences of faulty morality" (*zlonravie*). The comedy ends with a moral victory for the characters who represent virtue, and throughout the comedy there are references to virtue, seen as the result of proper education.

Fonvizin also made a significant contribution to the treatment of Russian serfs in that he depicts them in *Nedorosl'* as individuals. He jettisoned the conventional witty, intriguing servants, the comic caricatures and the "slaves content with their lot" who appeared in the plays of his contemporaries. By depicting them as individuals, Fonvizin emphasized the human aspect of his play and appealed to the feelings of his audience, stressing the moral lesson to be derived from it.

This appeal to the feelings and sensibility of audiences is to be seen in a number of other plays which introduce peasantry. When playwrights depict serfs on the stage, they frequently emphasise the benevolent relations existing between master and serfs. Satire is replaced by sentiment in such plays as Plavil'ščikov's *Bobyl'* ("The Landless Peasant", 1790), in which the peasants address their owner as "angel". The Princess in Kop'ev's *Obraščennyj mizantrop* (1794) is a woman of great sensibility, who rhapsodizes over her peasants as "a new race of mankind, who love me sincerely" (II, 3). The domestic servants in Šaxovskoj's *Urok koketkam* (1815) – twenty years after Kop'ev – are depicted sharing a paternal-filial relationship with their masters and mistresses. Xolmskij reminds the servant-girl Saša "Your father was my friend – not a servant" (I, 1), and the familiarity of the devoted serf Semeon towards Xolmskij is emphasized on several occasions.

The peasantry also make their appearance in many of the comic operas, a genre which flourished after the success in 1772 of Popov's *Anjuta*. But satire was even more out of place in comic opera than in comedy proper, and the relations between masters and serfs are usually shown in an idyllic, idealised and sentimental light. Comic opera was not meant to be taken seriously, but even so it contributed in a small way to the continued presence on the Russian stage of peasantry and the serfs.

## VII

### *Education*

Education was a matter of particular concern to Catherine and Russian society as a whole as it was throughout Europe, and this is reflected in many satirical comedies of the period. Education had many ramifications; it was closely associated in the minds of Lukin and others with the problem of national identity, and its purpose was primarily to produce useful citizens capable of carrying out their duty towards the homeland. To Elagin and all the playwrights who formed his group, the theatre was primarily a means for educating audiences in their duties towards society. Education was not seen as the acquisition of knowledge for its own sake, nor as the training of intellect; its purpose was to instil virtue. Catherine made this viewpoint clear in her decree of 1766, appointing a commission to consider the serf laws, when she said: "If you wish to prevent crimes, then propagate enlightenment among the people." [58]

The moralising which is such an important element in Russian satirical comedy was almost exclusively directed towards the instilling and propagation of virtue, which in turn could best be obtained through appropriate education. When Catherine said that the Russian theatre was a "national school" of which she was "senior teacher", she believed that the lesson taught in this "school" was how best to lead a life that was virtuous and useful to the State.[59] Fonvizin shared this view of virtue and education when his Starodum insisted that virtue was more important than intellect, and Pravdin declared that if all classes of people obtained an appropriate education, this would counteract "faulty morality" (*Ned.*, IV, 2 and V, 1).

Peter the Great had also been concerned with education although the purpose of his reforms differed from Catherine's in that they were essentially practical. Peter's decrees of 1714 and later, making education compulsory for the nobility and gentry, had been part of his plans for modernising the administration of the State, army and navy. For this, Peter required men with "at least the rudiments of a practical education".[60] But "the obligation to learn, go to school and pass ex-

---

[58]   *Ibid.*, p. 142.
[59]   L. Ja. Gurevič, *Istorija russkogo teatral'nogo byta*, I (Moscow, 1934), p. 97.
[60]   M. Raeff, "Home, school and service in the life of the eighteenth-century Russian nobleman", *Slavonic and East European Review*, 40 (1962), p. 299.

aminations in order to be considered legally of age did not at first suit the average nobleman, who strongly resisted it. In some cases the resistance persisted until late in the eighteenth century".[61] Examples of this resistance and satire aimed against the results of Peter's reforms as manifested during Catherine's reign occur in a number of comedies written after 1765.

Catherine was particularly concerned during the early part of her reign with the advantages of boarding-school education over domestic education at the hand of serf or foreign tutors. She depicted the deplorable results of a domestic education in the heroine of *O Vremja!*, who has been taught reading and writing by her grandmother's maid. In the 1760s, Catherine established two boarding-schools – the Smolnyj Institute for girls of genteel birth, and the *Vospitatel'nyj dom*. The purpose of these schools was to "remove and isolate pupils from their traditional environment, from barbarous and uneducated serf tutors and from insufficiently westernised families, in order to be better able to fashion the children" in ways that suited Catherine's own purposes.[62] In 1775, Catherine issued her Regulation for the administration of the *gubernii*, which included legislation for providing schools and regular inspection to "root out superstition, debauchery and corruption" from them.[63]

Public interest in education and particularly in its deficiencies and faults was equally great. Education was a favourite topic in the satirical journals. In 1782 Novikov and his followers founded a "Friendly Educational Society" supported by public contributions, which was able to provide grants for poor students, facilitate the publication of books and pay for students to visit Western Europe. In 1784 he established his "Typographical Company" in Moscow, also intended to contribute to the cause of education in Russia. Catherine did not approve of this private enterprise, but it forced her to persist in attempts at reforming the educational system of the country as a whole. In 1786, her Regulations for the national schools came into force, and a decade later some 8,000 pupils were attending these schools. But this was a tiny proportion of the thirty million population of the country, and by 1810 Xavier de Maistre was complaining to Razumovskij, Minister for National Education, that "despite the vast expenditures

[61] *Ibid.*, p. 299.
[62] *Ibid.*, p. 300.
[63] K. V. Sivkov, "Častnye pansiony i školy Moskvy v 80-x godax XVIII-ogo veka", *Istoričeskij arxiv*, VI (1951), p. 315.

of the government, the national schools remain empty .... we see this in the Gymnasiums, which keep having to close for want of pupils".[64]

The teachers themselves were chiefly to blame for this state of affairs. Since 1740 foreign tutors of French or German origin were regularly employed by the Russian nobility and gentry to educate their children, both in the capitals and provinces. When Catherine's commission inspected schools and pensions in Moscow in 1785, all the directors and teachers were found to be foreigners.[65] These foreigners were often of dubious origin, poorly educated and unable to provide their pupils with more than a superficial knowledge of the French language and French manners.[66] They were also notorious for the contempt they felt towards everything Russian, and they often succeeded in instilling this contempt into their Russian pupils. A contemporary declared that "the Russians, nearly all educated by the French, contract from infancy a marked predilection for this nation. Soon they know its language and history better than their own, and – having no homeland – France becomes the homeland of their hearts and imaginations." [67]

Not, however, that all the foreign tutors were bad. Catherine herself invited the eminent French philosopher d'Alembert as tutor to her son Paul and later employed a Swiss free-thinker La Harpe to educate her grandsons, despite his "republican views".[68] After the French Revolution a number of genuinely cultivated Frenchmen arrived in Russia and found employment as tutors. But the less well-to-do gentry failed to obtain the services of the competent domestic tutors, partly because their own faulty education prevented them from selecting efficient tutors, and partly because they could not afford to pay wages like those earned by such eminent scholars as Granmont, who received 25,000 roubles as tutor in the Dolgorukij household, or Bruckner, paid 35,000 roubles by the Kurakin family for educating the young princes.[69]

[64]   Quoted by V. Pokrovskij, *N. I. Novikov* (Moscow, 1910), p. 80.
[65]   K. V. Sivkov, *op. cit.*, p. 316.
[66]   Novikov reported in 1769 the arrival of a "ship from Bordeaux with twenty-four Frenchmen on board, all claiming to be barons, chevaliers, marquis and grafs ... Many are in difficulties with the Parisian police, who invited them to leave that city ... They intend to become teachers and domestic tutors of young, well-born persons", quoted in A. Afanas'jev, *Russkie satiričeskie žurnaly* (Moscow, 1859), p. 185.
[67]   C. P. F. Masson, *Mémoires secrets sur la Russie*, I (Paris, 1804), p. 164.
[68]   M. M. Štrange, *Russkoe obščestvo i francuzskaja revoljucija 1789-1794* (Moscow, 1956), p. 36.
[69]   C. P. F. Masson, *op. cit.*, p. 141.

Nevertheless, the fashion for employing a foreign domestic tutor or governess was too prevalent in Russian society for the poorer gentry to resist the temptation of engaging such persons as ex-coachmen or "actresses" to bring up their children.

The practice of sending children and adolescents abroad for an education meant that "the streets, cafes and restaurants of Paris were the real university of the Russian gentry" particularly in the 1760s.[70] The fashion prevailed throughout Catherine's reign and declined only in 1790, when Catherine ordered all the Russians in France to return home.

The results of this foreign education, whether at home or abroad, were that many Russians were "unable to write two lines in their own language without errors", and French became the language in which they preferred to read, write and converse in society.[71]

Four of the comedies produced in the 1764-65 season in St.-Petersburg dealt with various aspects of education. Sumarokov, who was opposed to the introduction of foreign teachers into Russia, expressed this in his *Pridanoe obmanom* ("A Dowry by Deceit"); here Mirsan is accused of "heresy" for having his children taught "pagan languages". The play also contained satirical references to secular schools. Lukin's *Ščepetil'nik* depicts several characters who are held up to ridicule as examples of harmful foreign education. They are displayed for the benefit of Čistoserdov's young nephew, who has been brought to see them "not for diversion, but as useful to your mind and heart" (sc. 1). Elagin's comedy *Jean de Mole, ili russkij parižanin* ("The Russian Parisian") is now lost, but the *Dramatičeskij slovar'* of 1787 described it as "a comedy castigating the foolishness of parents who send their children abroad to acquire a foreign education, although the children often return to Russia despising their own language".[72] A. G. Karin's *Rossijane vozvrativšiesja iz Francii* ("Russians Returning from France") contrasts two young men Blagorazumov and Pustorečin, both of whom have been educated in France, although only the former obtained benefit from his stay, while Pustorečin has become a "cosmopolitan fop".

Fonvizin's preoccupation with the topic of education is reflected in all his plays. The early version of *Nedorosl'*, tentatively dated as the

---

[70]  V. O. Ključevskij, *Kurs russkoj istorii*, pt. 5 (Moscow, 1937), p. 184.
[71]  V. Desnickij, "Prednosylki razvitija russkoj literatury v konce XVIII-ogo veka", in his *Izbrannye stat'i* (Moscow-Leningrad, 1958), pp. 76-77.
[72]  V. Desnickij, *op. cit.*, p. 77.

early 1760s,[73] contrasts the minor Ivanuška with Milovid, three years
his junior, who has already studied "German, French and Italian languages, arithmetic, geometry, trigonometry, architecture, history, ge-
ography, military subjects and the playing of various musical instru-
ments". Milovid has been educated at an official boarding-school,
whereas Ivanuška has received a domestic education and, at the age
of 20, is still ignorant of *gramota* (reading and writing). The first act
contains an examination scene, which derides the traditional "question
and answer" method of tuition, deriving from the Catechism and much
used by domestic tutors. The "raisonneur" of the play, Dobroljubov,
represents the views of those of the gentry who were aware of the
importance of education; he emphasizes the advantages Milovid has
acquired from the educational institutions established by Catherine to
remove children from the family influences which have spoiled
Ivanuška.

Fonvizin's *Brigadir,* written between 1766 and 1769, is thematically
close to the early *Nedorosl'*. Here, the harmful consequences of foreign
education are illustrated in Ivan, the Brigadir's son, who admires
everything French and despises everything Russian. He was "educated
by a French coachman" to whom he owes his "love for everything
French" (V, 2). Fonvizin's own view of French tutors of this kind is
revealed in Ivan's unexpected comment: "You know what our French
tutors are like ... The greater part of them are ignorant of reading
and writing ... A young man is like wax. If I had the misfortune to
fall in with a Russian who loved his own nation, then perhaps I would
not have been as I am" (V, 2). These remarks are so inappropriate to
Ivan's character that they can only have been Fonvizin's own views.

The ignorant domestic tutors themselves appear in Fonvizin's
*Nedorosl'* (1782), where the "minor" Mitrofan is yet another example
of the domestic education Catherine hoped to abolish. His ignorance
is exposed in another "question and answer" examination scene (IV,
8). Both this full-length play and the earlier version of *Nedorosl'*,
though it is merely a sketch, provide Fonvizin's most satirical comments
on the result of Peter the Great's schemes for the compulsory education of young gentry. Mitrofan's exclamation: "I want to marry, not
study!" is a direct reference to Peter's legislation, which had prohibited young men under age from marrying until their education
was completed. Both comedies imply that Peter's legislation was pro-

---

[73]  V. N. Vsevolodskij-Gerngross, *Russkij teatr vtoroj poloviny XVIII veka*
(Moscow, 1960), pp. 60, 366-375 summarises the evidence.

ducing almost worthless results under Catherine, since the compulsory education could be – and usually was – obtained at the hands of serf or foreign tutors, like those engaged in the education of Mitrofan. Fonvizin thus satirised in *Nedorosl'* both the faulty education of the gentry, and the results of this faulty education, which made the gentry cruel and tyrannical to their serfs and consequently unworthy of being gentry.

In his later unfinished plays and sketches for unwritten plays, Fonvizin continued to satirise faulty education in general and foreign tutors in particular. The sketch *Vybor guvernera* ("Choice of a Tutor", 1785) contrasts a Russian tutor Nel'stecov with a French tutor Pelikan, to the disadvantage of the latter. The French coachman responsible for Ivan's Gallomania in *Brigadir* is referred to again in the sketch *Dobryj nastavik* ("A Good Preceptor", 1790), where doubts are cast upon his moral qualities as well as his educational capacity. *Gofmejster* is lost, but appears by its title to have been concerned with the same topic as the other plays and sketches.

That Fonvizin's contemporaries were equally interested in the faulty education of the gentry as a topic for satirical comedy is attested by the imitations and sequels which followed *Nedorosl'*. They included Plavil'ščikov's *Sgovor Kutejkina* ("Kutejkin's Agreement", 1789), in which the characters Skotinin, Cyfirkin, Eremeevna and Kutejkin himself all re-appear; Kop'ev's *Obraščennyj mizantrop* ("The Misanthrope Converted", 1794) which depicts Fonvizin's positive character Pravdin disillusioned by the falsity of society; the anonymous *Ženix bit i dovolen* ("The Betrothed Beaten yet Pleased", 1795); Goročaninov's *Mitrofanuška v otstavke* ("Mitrofanuška in Retirement", 1800), which portrays more absurd domestic tutors of the type mocked in *Nedorosl'*, while the leading female character Demosedova is a "zlaja furija" like Mrs. Prostakova.

The first of these imitations, and the closest, was Kropotov's *Fomuška babuškin vnuček* ("Fomuška Granny's Boy", 1785). The title echoes Skotinin's remark: "Ja sestrin brat", Prostakov's "Ja ženin muž" and Mitrofan's "Ja mamuškin synok" (*Ned.*, III, 5). Fomuška, the ignorant "granny's boy" is subjected to a "question and answer" examination of the catechism kind, which exposes his ignorance (I, 4). Fomuška's tutor is a badly-educated hypocrite, who was expelled from a seminary, but now finds domestic tutoring an excellent way of lining his own pockets at the expense of his employers.

Catherine caricatured domestic tutors both Russian and foreign. A person described only as "the teacher of Vestnikova's grandson" appears in *Gospoža Vestnikova s sem'eju* as a ridiculous pedant, who has taught the unfortunate child to echo French phrases, which no one else in the household understands. Vestnikova cries: "Whatever does the child mean? How I long to drive this nuisance out of my house!" (indicating the teacher). As soon as she can replace him, he will "go back to being coachman again". This child has been seen as a prototype of Fonvizin's "minor".[74] The scene in which his tutor questions the boy certainly suggests he will grow up to be another Ivan (the son of Fonvizin's Brigadir), with all his admiration for everything French.

Catherine's early plays also refer to education in a more general way. The bigoted Mrs. Čudakina rails against modern education: "Nowadays they teach young girls all sorts of thing in 'Piter'" (*O Vremja!*), and Catherine castigates the reactionaries who objected to female education by making Čudakina complain: "Had I a daughter, I'd have less trouble. Why teach a girl *gramota*? The less a girl knows, the less she will lie" (III, 3). This attitude towards education is echoed in the anonymous *Podražatel'* ("The Imitator", 1779): Skopidomova, an elderly lady, protests: "Ah, you see what comes of teaching a girl accursed *gramota*! Never teach a girl to read or write – the consequences will be regrettable."

Other playwrights, too, refer to the faulty education of girls. Knjažnin's absurd Mrs. Lentjagina in *Čudaki* ("The Monstrosities", 1790) expatiates on the genteel upbringing of her daughter, Ulinka, the play's heroine. Ulinka "does not know how to sew or weave, but leaves all that for low people. ... She speaks French like a mademoiselle, and would like to forget Russian entirely" (II, 2). Both the heroine and her maid in Kop'ev's *Obraščennyj mizantrop* were educated at the Smolnyj Institute for Well-born Girls, but in the heroine's case, the consequences are that she "weeps at the stupidities of her mother and father", has "learned German ways", and writes a letter in grotesque French, which other characters deride (I, 6).

Catherine's later comedies (after 1785) include caricatures of foreign tutors who are not only ignorant, but dishonest. The French tutor Roti and Mme. Grybuž, governess of the heroine in *Obmanščik* are examples of the worst kind of foreign domestic tutors: Roti "spent a year making his living in public inns" before being engaged as tutor in the Samblin household. Mme. Grybuž elopes with the charlatan Xalifalxžerston,

---

[74]  Kallaš and Efros, *op. cit.*, p. 328.

taking Samblin's diamonds with her (V, 4). The tutor of young Ivan Igotin in her *Nedorazumenie* is described in the *dramatis personae* as a "flatterer, pedant and hypocrite, and is caricatured whenever he appears: he utters tedious aphorisms which other characters mock, and insists on reading a preposterous 'mythological play' of his own composition" (III, 6).

## Gallomania

Because social conditions underwent a number of rapid changes towards the end of Catherine's reign, faulty education became a matter of less interest to playwrights, satirists and their audiences or readers. In any case, one of the main consequences of this faulty education had already proved a most rewarding theme for satirical comedy. This was Gallomania, itself a direct product of fashionable French education which had been allowed to develop and flourish in Russian society as a direct result of the educational system. Gallomania was so widespread in Russia that there is hardly a comedy between 1765 and 1823 which does not contain satirical references to it.

Gallomania was first satirised on the Russian stage by Sumarokov in his *Čudovišči* ("The Monstrosities", 1750) in which a young Russian exclaims: "Oh, why was I born a Russian? Oh, Nature! Art thou not ashamed of giving me a Russian father?" Later, he challenges another young man to a duel because the latter has addressed him as "a Russian and a brother". Another "petit-maître" appears in Sumarokov's *Ssora u muža* ("A Husband's Quarrel with a Wife", 1750), and was to provide a blue-print for all later ridicule in comedies and in the satirical journals for the "preposterous Franco-Russian jargon of polite society".[75] It was the "wide gap between their real natures and their appearance and conduct" that was to make "the fashion-plates of St.-Petersburg and Moscow such ready targets for satire".[76] By 1765, Gallomania was firmly established as a favourite target in comedy, and attacks upon its manifestations formed part of Lukin's campaign for greater national awareness in the theatre. In Lukin's view, there was a close connection between foreign influence or admiration of everything foreign, with immorality: he declared: "Morality

[75]   Bertha Malnick, review article of P. N. Berkov, *Russkaja komedija i komičeskaja opera*, in *Slavonic and East European Review*, 31 (1953), p. 574.
[76]   Hans Rogger, *National consciousness in eighteenth-century Russia* (Cambridge, Mass., 1961), p. 48.

is more easily found and preserved among those who have not accepted the fashionable and foreign-derived standards of behaviour." [77] Hence Gallomania was attacked by the playwrights because they believed that anyone afflicted by it was incapable of virtue.

At first Gallomania was satirised by reproducing or caricaturing the affected manners and vocabulary of the "petits-maîtres" and "giddy-pates". These creatures were epitomised in Ivan and the Sovetnitsa of Fonvizin's *Brigadir,* who use the exaggerated phraseology and vocabulary of the fops: "Hélas! de tout mon coeur . . . Dieu! Pardieu! . . . Ja indiferan vo vsem tom . . . Bez dissimjulacii . . ." and the like. Ivan declares: "I would like to have a wife with whom I could speak no other language but French. Our life then would be much happier" (I, 1). He complains that to be born Russian "is a *défaut* which it is *totalement* impossible to correct". The long-lasting popularity of *Brigadir,* indicated by its revival in 1812 and again in 1814, show that Gallomania was still a familiar phenomenon in Russian society.

By the end of the eighteenth century, however, satire against Gallomania had developed from mere satire of manners and vocabulary to satire castigating French influence in Russia on a wider scale. Catherine had been one of the first to see that French influence was more than merely a question of affectation in manners, dress and phraseology. Her Mrs. Čudakina declared (1772): "The world has gone awry since foreign learning was introduced by our enemies" into Russia (*O Vremja!* III, 3). French influence was blamed for a decline in the honesty of Russian merchants in Plavil'ščikov's *Sidelec* ("The Tapster", 1793), and a year later, a character in Levšin's *Svad'ba Boldyreva* ("Boldyrev's Nuptials", 1794) declared: "Affectionate and virtuous love no longer exist here . . . Messieurs the French have sown a fine harvest among us in Russia!"

Anti-French feeling was intensified by political events, which ranged from the French Revolution and execution of Louis XVI and the breaking-off of diplomatic relations in 1793, to the veerings and reversals in Russian policy towards Napoleon after 1800. Despite their French education and upbringing, Russian society became increasingly anti-French. Krylov's portrait of Mme. Kare, the modiste, in the comedy *Modaja lavka* ("The Fashionable Boutique", 1805) suggests something of this change in attitude: whereas the dishonest Mme. Grybuž in *Obmanščik* was absurd, Mme. Kare is both dishonest and immoral. She permits the hero Lestov to use her shop for an assignation with the

[77]  Quoted by Hans Rogger, *op. cit.,* p. 57.

heroine, "providing you pay me for my loss of reputation" (II, 12). A similar change occurred in Russian national awareness, which was replaced by patriotism; and the slavish imitators of French manners began to be contrasted with patriotic Russians, invariably to their dis-advantage.

### The "Philosophes" and the "Umniki"

From attacks on French immorality it was but a short step to satirical attacks on French ideas. However, satire against enlightened ideas and the philosophers who propagated them had already become a common-place on the French stage. The word "philosophe" became a term of derision as early as the 1750s, partly because "ces prétendus esprits forts" in fashionable society had degraded the word by indiscriminate use, and partly because of the number of satirical comedies attacking them.

One or more "philosophes" appeared in over 180 French comedies produced between the 1720s and the Revolution.[78] The purpose of these plays was to combat contemporary philosophical doctrines which seemed to threaten organised society. The leaders of enlightened thought – Voltaire, Rousseau, Diderot – were all attacked, often with personal caricature. Some of the characteristic traits of the "philosophe" as seen by the French playwrights were their "desire to write books, an ex-aggerated enthusiasm for England, an indiscriminate and pedantic search for knowledge, and the establishment of *bureaux d'esprit,* often by ladies with pretensions to intellect".[79]

First of the anti-philosophical playwrights in Russia was A. P. Sumarokov, who was also an innovator in a number of other ways. In addition to his attacks on individuals (pp. 17ff. above), Sumarokov broadened the scope of satire *na lico* to ridicule his rivals' ideas. His most celebrated attack in this vein was launched against the writer and literary theorist V. K. Tredjakovskij, who appears as Tresotinjus in the one-act farce of the same name (1750). He is bluntly described in the *dramatis personae* as "a pedant". This disagreeable epithet was often attached to "philosophes" in the French comedies.[80] Their in-discriminate pursuit of learning had been ridiculed from the start of

---

[78]   Ira O. Wade, *The "Philosophe" in eighteenth-century French comedy* (Princeton, 1926), iv.
[79]   *Ibid.,* p. 97.
[80]   *Ibid.,* pp. 97, 102.

the "anti-philosophe" movement in the 1720s. The incongruous subjects which pedantic philosophers studied included the language of
birds, magnetism, astrology, volcanoes and the philosopher's stone.

Sumarokov's farce *Tresotinjus* depicts an elderly gentleman Oront,
who has been deluded by the pedant's parade of learning. He hopes to
marry off his daughter Klarisa to Tresotinjus. This situation of a parent
deluded by the claims of a philosopher into giving him his or her
daughter's hand in marriage occurs in a number of the French comedies.[81] When Tresotinjus appears on the stage, Sumarokov provides
him with turns of speech and stylistic mannerisms to help the audience
identify him with Tredjakovskij. The pedant pays court to Klarisa by
reading her a song "in trochaic metres", and boasts that although the
song appears simple to most people, he can prove "by argument" that
it is nothing of the sort (scene 3). A favourite method of ridiculing a
philosopher was to have him fall in love and expose himself to derision
as a "philosophe amoureux".

Tresotinjus is joined by a second pedant, Bobembjus, perhaps a
caricature of Empress Anna's Court philosopher Kirjak Kondratovič.[82]
Bobembius accosts Tresotinjus with a series of ludicruous syllogisms,
parodying the scholastic philosophy of Leibnitz, Wolff and others,
according to which anything could be demonstrated as logically as a
problem in geometry. Bobembius informs Klarisa that he "despises
pleasure, amusement and beauty", often a trait of philosophers on the
French stage. He reveals he is a professor of antiquities, and possesses
a "drinking glass made before the Deluge, the cup Semiramis drank
from, and a needle, once the property of Ahusuerus" (scene 6). The two
philosophers embark upon a learned dispute as to the "shape of the
hard sign", which becomes heated, though conducted in pompous and
scholastic terminology. They are interrupted by the *miles gloriosus*
Bramabral, who drives both from the stage.

Sumarokov is deriding Tredjakovskij's theories of versification and
his "pedantry", and makes it clear that Tresotinjus-Tredjakovskij is
personally "a man of honour, and with that we have no quarrel".
Sumarokov pointedly disclaims any personal malice or spite against
Tredjakovskij's moral character. He renewed the attack against his
rival's ideas in *Tretejnij sud,* later re-titled *Čudovišči* when Sumarokov

---

[81] Such as Palissot's *Le Cercle* (1755), Cailleau's *Les Originaux* (1760), and
other plays summarised by Professor Wade, *op. cit.*
[82] P. N. Berkov, *Aleksandr Petrovič Sumarokov 1717-1777* (Leningrad, 1949),
p. 60.

revised it for performance in the late 1760s. Now he introduces the pedant Kriticiondjus, who claims to speak Greek and suffers from Gallomania. This is the Russian counterpart of the French philosophers' excessive love for England. Kriticiondjus boasts of having written "twelve volumes *in folio* on a song 'Prosti, moj svet!' not to mention 'six dozen epigrams on *Xorev*', and 'ninety-nine satires in the Syrian language against those who produce Russian tragedies'". This fondness for writing enormous books and satirical poetry was yet another characteristic of the French philosophers, who were commonly depicted on the stage as men of letters afflicted with graphomania.

The later title of this play, *Čudovišči,* coincides with the sub-title of Palissot's notorious *le Cercle, ou les Originaux* of 1755. This was a *comédie-parade* attacking Jean-Jacques Rousseau, first performed before Stanislas Poniatowski at Nancy, which created a six-month scandal in the literary world, well documented by Grimm in his correspondence. However, no textual analogies occur between Palissot's comedy and that of Sumarokov.

Sumarokov's *Narciss* (1750) bears the name of a philosopher who appeared in the first of the French anti-philosopher comedies – du Cerceau's *Philosophe à la mode,* first produced in Paris in 1720. The comedy was not printed, but a 50-page article on it appeared in the *Mercure de France* in June, 1720, and the play was very celebrated. Du Cerceau's main target was the Helvetian doctrine of self-interest, and although Sumarokov does not call his Narciss a philosopher or pedant, this character also carries self-interest to an extreme.

In these three slight plays, Sumarokov depicts a number of traits considered typical of the philosophers of the contemporary French theatre: their names are of Latin or Greek derivation, just as the philosophes were named Theophrastus, Dortidjus, Rectiligre, and the like: they lay claim to vast abstruse learning, and write monstrous books: they are fond of scholastic logic and theorise about literature: their Gallomania echoes the Anglomania of their French counterparts.

Sumarokov's son-in-law Ja. B. Knjažnin did not – as far as we know – introduce characters *na lico* into his own comedies. Perhaps he suffered too much at the hand of Krylov. However, philosophers play leading roles in two of his comedies. The three-act *Neudačnij primiritel'* ("The Unsuccessful Mediator", 1785) introduces a "philosophical cook", one Jakov Roster, who boasts he has learned to regard everything "through philosophical eyes", thanks to the teachings of a certain Monsieur Casserole. In Roster's eyes, "gastronomy combines all fields of knowledge – from astronomy, physics, chemistry and ethics to politics and medicine" (I, 1). Now Knjažnin introduces another philosopher named Sinexdoxos, a believer in the "power of argument and logic". He falls in love with the maid-servant Marina because of her skill in "rhetorical similes and hypotheses". Sinexdoxos sets out to prove by argument that "today everyone is stupider than the ancients – with the exception of myself" (II, 5), and he writes an "exordium" addressed to Marina, copiously adorned with mythological names and tropes, composed "strictly according to the rules of poetics".

Despite his pretentions to learning, Sinexdoxos is soon exposed as a fraudulent "soi-disant" philosopher with no Greek and less Latin. Alarmed lest the philosophical cook Roster betray him, Sinexdoxos takes comfort in strong drink, on the principle that "we learned people are but little interested in food". Finally, Roster drags his rival into the kitchen, where "they both sit by the fire and mourn the corrupt manners of mankind" (III, 7). The fraudulent philosopher, of which species Sinexdoxos is a particularly outrageous specimen, was one of the stock types in the French comedies. Many of the stage philosophers also had a strongly misanthropic strain in their characters, and can be heard frequently complaining that the world is peopled by fools and evil-doers.

Knjažnin returned to the attack on foolish philosophers in *Čudaki*, the title of which echoes Sumarokov's *Čudovišči*. The date of Knjažnin's comedy is uncertain, but he may have written it in 1790.[83] The central character is Mr. Lentjagin, whose "speaking name" indicates he represents the idle species of philosopher often caricatured on the French stage. He is described in the *dramatis personae* as "a man who philosophises in his own way", but his philosophy is merely a façade to cover his sloth. He complains, for instance, that putting on clothes with their "loops and knots, which the world invented", leaves him no time for "thinking". His philosophy embraces an admiration for "simple behaviour", and indifference for money, both traits illustrated in his attitude towards the valet Prolaz. Lentjagin quotes Seneca, whose aim in life (he believes) was to attain "imperturbability of mind". Lentjagin has attained so much that he lets his wife lie in a swoon while he carries on a long conversation with somebody else.

Lentjagin tries to convert his valet Prolaz to "philosophy". A fondness for proselytising on behalf of their own notions was characteristic of the French stage philosophers, many of whom succeed – at least

[83]   Ja. B. Knjažnin, *Izbrannye proizvedenija* (Leningrad, 1961), p. 738.

temporarily – in converting their valets. Indeed, the "valet-philosophe" was himself a stock figure on the eighteenth-century stage in Paris.[84] Lentjagin persuades Prolaz that "anyone who is honest is my equal in every thing", and insists upon Prolaz being seated and wearing a hat in his master's presence. He even urges Prolaz to address him as "ty".[85] Prolaz naturally declines at first, then realises – like his French proto-types – that he may be able to profit by his master's notions. He obeys, whereupon Lentjagin embraces him and begs to be his "friend".

The plot of *Čudaki* turns upon Lentjagin's fondness for philosophy. He decides to marry his daughter Ulin'ka to the valet philosopher Prolaz, but the latter sees it will be more to his advantage to support the courtship of Ulin'ka by the hero Prijat. He therefore advises Prijat to adopt the "pastoral name" of Semeon, and to claim he is a phi-losopher who seeks to marry in order to "bring up a whole family of enlightened persons, and entirely change the world". Prolaz also per-suades Lentjagin that it is his "duty" to bestow Ulin'ka's hand on the "most philosophical" of her rival suitors. Prijat succeeds in winning her, and Prolaz is suitably rewarded with the serving-maid's hand in marriage.

Knjažnin takes as his target in both these comedies the soi-disant philosophe who protests a devotion to philosophy out of vanity, idle-ness, ostentation or personal advantage, and in this respect the plays closely resemble the French comedies which deride these attributes.

Catherine's second group of comedies, already discussed in terms of attacks on individuals, also illustrate the manner in which play-wrights attack ideas. Early in her reign, Catherine had admired and encouraged the philosophers of the French Age of Enlightenment. Her correspondence with Voltaire, her generosity towards Rousseau, and her meetings with Diderot in 1773-1774 are well documented.[86] But by the 1780s, her admiration had evaporated, even though the phi-losophes were no longer regarded in their homeland as an important threat to the established order. Catherine now turned her attention to a species which seemed to her much more dangerous – the Freemasons.

At this time, Masonry was well entrenched in Moscow, where Novikov opened his printing-house in May 1779. He had been a Mason since mid-1775, when he entered the Astrea Lodge,[87] and he played a

[84] Ira O. Wade, *op. cit.*, p. 21.
[85] Similar scenes occur in Palissot's *Le Cercle* and other "anti-philosophe" plays.
[86] E.g. G. P. Gooch, *Catherine the Great and other studies* (London, 1954), and C. de Larivière, *Cathérine II et la Révolution française* (Paris, 1895).
[87] M. N. Longinov, *Novikov i moskovskie Martinisti* (Moscow, 1867), p. 100.

leading part in the movement. A number of other mystical and hermetical sects, closely associated with or deriving from Masonry, were in existence in St.-Petersburg and Moscow. They included the Martinists, followers of the teaching of Louis-Claude, Marquis de Saint-Martin. His treatise *Des Erreurs et de la Vérité* (1775) was significantly described on the title-page as "Par un Ph(ilosophe) Inc(onnu)".[88] Many Russian Freemasons were Rosicrucians, and indeed, most of the founders of Novikov's Typographical Company established in Moscow in 1784, belonged to this sect.[89] The mystical teachings of yet another popular and fashionable sect – the Theosophists – linked it with Masonry.

Catherine aimed three of her second group of comedies against these sects and their followers. Her *Obmanščik* attacks the Martinists, who are specifically referred to in the first scene. Their representative in the play is the "mystic" Xalifalkžerston, whose name echoes the Masonic fondness for foreign-sounding names. He is an alchemist, preoccupied with the manufacture of "pure gold" by chemical processes. This was a subject which greatly interested the Rosicrucians, who spent time and money in search of the "philosopher's stone" that could convert base metals into gold. They had nine ranks of alchemists in the sect. Novikov's printing-house issued several handbooks on alchemy, including the *Chemical Psalter* by the pseudo-Paracelsus which was published in the same year as Catherine's *Obmanščik,* and was immediately confiscated by the Moscow authorities.

In the next comedy, *Obolščennyj,* Catherine derides the effect of "mysticism" on the play's central character, Radotov. "Mysticism" has turned him into an eccentric: he shuns "all that is good, cheerful or agreeable", and boasts of his "insensibility". His obsession with mysticism and occult philosophy has made his family miserable, but he protests: "What care I if my wife, children and friends all die? It will not affect me" (I, 6). Radotov's boasted insensibility foreshadows the stoical imperturbability of Lentjagin in *Čudaki.*

Radotov has made his house a rendezvous for other members of a mystical sect, all of whom are "poorly dressed, speak incomprehensible languages, and have pallid faces". Many of the French philosophes were depicted as poor, shabby and subsisting on the charity of a patron

[88] Ja. L. Barskov, *Perepiska moskovskix Masonov 1780-1792* (Petrograd, 1915), p. 292.
[89] G. V. Vernadskij, *Russkoe Masonstvo v carstvovanie Ekaterinoj II-oj* (Petrograd, 1917), p. 122.

or patroness.[90] The members of the sect hold a meeting in Radotov's house, and are watched through the key-hole by the maid-servant Praskov'ya. She takes their ceremonies as a game of blind-man's buff, and they emerge from the inner room tipsy.

At one point in the play, the hero declares that Radotov and his fellow-mystics are "trying to establish schools, hospitals and the like". In his view (which was also that of Catherine), such activities should be left to government legislation, not to private individuals. Catherine's mistrust of Novikov's philanthropic activities is clearly expressed in this speech: and the meeting at Radotov's house may point directly to the meetings Novikov arranged at a house in St.-Petersburg, rented for the purpose.[91]

Catherine told Grimm that her *Šaman sibirskij* (1786) was designed as "un coup de massif pour les Enthousiastes". The sect is represented by several honest but gullible Russians deluded by the "Siberian magician" Amban-Laj, who has been introduced into St.-Petersburg society by Bobin. Amban-Laj wastes no time in converting Bobin and his friends to such beliefs as "Silence is a method for obtaining Non-being", "Love and rage have but one origin, like salt, mineral oil and density", or "There are two forces in all bodies – one elemental, one physical: to cure an illness, we must drive out or increase one force or the other" (II, 5). But the magician is finally exposed as a charlatan, and arrested for "promising to conjure up the late husband of a widow, keeping a school for magicians, and telling fortunes for money" (V, 2).

Catherine had more reason to ridicule mystics, Freemasons and the like than Sumarokov to deride Tredjakovskij's literary theories, or Knjažnin to mock philosophising as a foible of idle gentry. The cosmopolitan associations of Masonry were strong in the 1770s and 1780s, and Catherine had good reason to fear them. Her use of stage-plays as a means for combatting her enemies illustrates the prestige of comedy as a genre in eighteenth-century Russia.

Russian Masonry never recovered Novikov's arrest in 1792, and the sentence of 15 years imprisonment passed upon him (although he was released in 1796). Caricatures of philosophers and alchemists almost entirely disappear from the stage after this date. Klušin's *Alximist* (1792) while deriding the search for the philosopher's stone, the elixir of life and other Rosicrucian notions, is merely a one-act tour-de-force, with little satire.

[90] Ira O. Wade, *op. cit.*, pp. 66-67.
[91] M. N. Longinov, *op. cit.*, p. 98.

However, many Decembrists dabbled in Freemasonry, and the sect forms a direct link between them and such eighteenth-century figures as Novikov, Radiščev and the Rosicrucians. The sect underwent a revival after the Napoleonic wars, and its associations with philosophers and philosophising may have contributed to the sudden reappearance of the species in the comedies of Šaxovskoj and Zagoskin. Now, however, they are called "umniki", although many of their characteristics recall those of the early philosophers – including their fancied intellectual superiority to the rest of society, their liberal views, an exaggerated desire to write books, their indiscriminate search for knowledge, and their "bureaux d'esprit" for the display of wit and intellect.

The first "modnyj umnik" appeared on the Russian stage in 1815, and the leading exponent of satirical attacks against the type was A. A. Šaxovskoj, the conservative director of the Imperial theatres since 1802. His *Urok koketkam* ("A Lesson for Flirts") furnishes a detailed portrait of the type in Ol'gin, who has been advised to visit Lipec Spa to cure his "disordered nerves, migraines and vertigo" which he "brought back from Paris, along with the right to decry everything and esteem no one" (I, 3). Other traits which relate Ol'gin to the petits-maîtres of the eighteenth century include the "empty education often given to the sons of eminent noblemen". When a conversation turns on "our antiquities, Russian laws, the advantages of the country where he was born ... he at once begins yawning". His conversation consists largely of "improper couplets by French authors, and free-thinking nonsense", for which, however, he is "considered agreeable in society" (*ib.*).

Šaxovskoj introduces two more young men of Ol'gin's generation in his play. They represent genuine "um" as opposed to the false values and affectations of the "modnyj umnik" Ol'gin. Both Xolmskij and Pronskij are virtuous and patriotic: Xolmskij lives according to advice given him by his grandfather, which echoes the advice given by the "raisonneurs" of eighteenth-century comedy: "Always be yourself, do not hope to please everyone, go straight ahead in life, do not value gossip and always respect the judgement of the society in which you live, though without accepting all its tittle-tattle with unnecessary enthusiasm ..." (I, 3). Xolmskij displays a benevolent, paternal attitude towards serfs which makes him worthy of being gentry.

The contrast between genuinely "umnye liudi" and the "umniki" which Šaxovskoj emphasized in *Urok koketkam* was also stressed in Zagoskin's portayals of "umniki" in his comedies *Russkij pustynik*

("The Russian Hermit", 1817) and *Bogatonov* (1817). The "umnik" Miroslavskij in *Bogatonov* thus describes some of the qualities of his own species: "He must speak with contempt of his own literature, which he does not know, and praise foreign literature which he does not understand" (III, 1). Just as Šaxovskoj's Ol'gin was depicted as a malicious gossip, so Zagoskin's "umnik" Vel'skij in the comedy *Dobryj malyj* ("The Good Fellow", 1820) is an intriguer and cheat, although his qualities of "um" have brought him the reputation in society of a "good fellow".

As well as attacking "umniki" infected with foreign notions, Šaxovskoj also derided pseudo-pedantry, which had been another target of the French anti-philosophical comedies. In *Pustodomy* ("Empty-houses", 1819), the central character is Radugin, a philosopher who plans to publish an "economic-philosophical journal". The contents of this journal are to be "borrowed from economists, encyclopedias, journals and the *Moniteur universel*" – the official publication of the French government. Radugin's preoccupation with this journal leads him to neglect his household and estate and he is only saved from ruin by an elderly uncle, who shows him the error of his ways. Zagoskin's sequel to this play was *Bogatonov v derevne* (1821), in which another philosopher is ridiculed for his "liberal" ideas regarding the management of his estate and the well-being of his serfs.

The "desire to write books, the indiscriminate search for knowledge and the establishment of 'bureaux d'esprit' " which were characteristic traits of the French "philosophes" spread into Russian society and were satirised on the stage after 1815. Zagoskin's *Večerinka učenyx* ("The Scholars" Soirée, 1819) derides the blue-stocking widow Radugina, who plans to issue a literary journal, occupies herself with all kinds of ill-assorted sciences, and holds a "soirée" at which third-rate poets and hack journalists quarrel among themselves. Zagoskin also depicted a "dreadful philosopher" in his Mr. Landyšev, in *Derevenskij filozof* ("A Village Philosopher", 1822). Landyšev "once published a political book" and claims on the strength of it to "despise fame, glory and wealth" while extorting taxes from his serfs and he "will do anything for a smile from an eminent person" (sc. 3).

All the satirical comedies of Šaxovskij and Zagoskin aimed against the "umniki" were didactic in purpose. In this respect they conform closely to the predominant trend of eighteenth-century comedy. However, didacticism in the theatre was opposed in the early 1800s by the "haute comédie" known as "blagorodnaja komedija" adapted from

French salon comedies. The "blagorodnaja komedija" is discussed in more detail in Chapter III, and all that need be said of it here is that such comedies were devoid of the moralising and social satire in the Russian topics handled by Šaxovskoj and his admirers. It was the opposition between satirical and "blagorodnaja" comedy which paved the way for a social comedy based on Russian themes and manners, in which the unfashionable didactic element was less emphatic, while the dialogue and situations were as witty and ingenious as those of "blagorodnaja komedija". This play was Griboedov's *Gore ot uma,* which epitomises many of the eighteenth-century traditions while revealing them in a new light. Griboedov's original use of these traditions is apparent, for instance, in his handling of the "umnik" theme. To his predecessors Šaxovskoj and Zagoskin, "um" was either genuine or false: the "um" on which fashionable *umniki* prided themselves was essentially false, in that it was a suspect quality connected with free-thinking, dangerous foreign notions and general affectation coupled with lack of genuine feeling. Their portraits of the *umniki* depict affected, malicious, frivolous, egoistical young men. Their own sympathies lay with the patriotic, dutiful and virtuous young men whose intellect had not been affected by foreign ideas or manners.

Griboedov's portrait of Čackij is diametrically opposed to those of Šaxovskoj and the others. His hero displays a number of traits common to the fashionable *umniki* – his attitude towards Russian society is, on the whole, satirical, he has spent three years abroad, even the fact that he is unmarried. But in *Gore ot uma* Čackij as positive hero is contrasted not with a virtuous Xolmskij but with the hypocritical, time-serving Molčalin. Griboedov also sets up Čackij against the conventional, patriarchal and conservative groups of characters in the play. In this respect, Griboedov was giving voice to the despair of genuinely intellectual young Russians of the 1820s, who found themselves confronted with "le vieux credo de l'impénitente noblesse", and the "void which is the life of St.-Petersburg, listening to the mutterings of the old who praise the past, and condemn each step ahead".[92]

Significantly, *Gora ot uma* ends with the defeat and flight of Čackij. This reveals the extent of the gap separating Griboedov's genuinely *umnyj* hero from the *umniki* derided by Šaxovskij. For in the latter's *Kakadu* ("The Cockatoo", 1820) – a sequel to *Urok koketkam* – Ol'gin and the fashionable coquette Leleva who quit society because they no

[92]   Quoted by Charles Quenet, *Tchaadaev et les lettres philosophiques* (Paris, 1931), p. 24.

longer had a place in it, suggest five years later that they may after all be able to return to it. The conclusion of *Gore ot uma*, on the other hand, implies that although Griboedov was sympathetic towards the genuinely intelligent and liberal *umnyj* young man in Russian society, he divined that there was in reality no place for the species in this society, and that it was doomed to disappear. In fact, a "Famusov" was to become the Minister for National Education in 1825,[93] and the Decembrist revolt also marked the end of the period in which the young men endowed with genuine "um" had flourished.

[93] V. Ivanov-Razumnik, *Istorija russkoj obščestvennoj mysli*, I (St.-Petersburg, 1908), p. 134.

## II.  CHARACTERS

### The Personification of Vices

Although many eighteenth-century playwrights used satire to attack individuals, the main purpose of their comedies was always to castigate vices or foibles which the writers hoped to abolish from their own society. To attain this end, they set up targets a gallery of characters who personified these vices or foibles, and proceeded to ridicule them. Thus a writer seeking to satirise bigotry would construct a personage in which were incorporated as many aspects of bigotry as possible. The writers were not particularly concerned with whether this personage bore any resemblance to a human being. The figure they constructed was a vice personified, a set of generalisations upon a vice or foible, a lay figure ruled "by some extravagant habit, passion or affection . . . by the oddness of which he is immediately distinguished".[1] This fondness for generalisation and abstraction when dealing with "Man" was moreover in keeping with the eighteenth-century attitude towards the human race; to writers of the time, the "abstract man stood in the foreground, the individual in the background".[2]

The depiction of personified vices was facilitated by models provided in foreign satirical comedy. Plays by such admired writers as Molière and his successors furnished the Russian playwrights with all the elements they required for constructing a comedy that would both instruct and divert their audiences. In addition to stereotyped plots, the French models also provided a gallery of equally stereotyped protagonists: they included a raisonneur to point the all-important moral and act as spokesman for the author: a hero and heroine: one or more unsuccess-

---

[1] John Dryden, *Of dramatic poesy*, ed. by George Watson (London, 1962), p. 73.
[2] V. Ivanov-Razumnik, *Istorija russkoj obščestvennoj mysli*, 2nd ed., I (St.-Petersburg, 1908), p. 33.

ful suitor's for the heroine's hand: a parent or guardian to provide obstacles to the hero's suit: and a group of secondary characters ranging from hack poets to peasant match-makers and fortune-tellers.

This handful of figures populated Russian comedy for over half a century. Not until Puškin were Russian dramatists "profoundly exercised by the problem of creating dramatic character".[3] Yet the gallery served the eighteenth-century writers' purposes very well, and indeed offered them several advantages not to be gained by strikingly original or highly individualised creations. Their audiences could immediately recognise each character as they appeared on stage, in the same way that a Greek audience knew "as soon as ever they heard the name of Oedipus ... that he had killed his father by mistake".[4] The audience could instantly identify the hero, the heroine, the comic servant, the bad-tempered parent, and could place them within the intrigue of the play. Consequently, no time need be spent on identifying or explaining them, and thus occupying time that could more profitably be spent on moralising.

Attempts were made to russianise the stereotypes in the 1760s. Lukin, Fonvizin and their imitators introduced a number of characters representing specifically and recognisably Russian types. But their purpose was not to add "realism" for its own sake. The point of these Russian types in comedy was to bring home to the audiences that the vices and foibles satirised were those which afflicted the audiences themselves. As Lukin insisted, the use of foreign names or manners by Sumarokov, in his comedies of the 1750s, had suggested to the audiences that the targets of the plays were the foreigners he depicted, and that the satire had nothing to do with Russian reality.

At first, the Russian types introduced into comedies were episodic. Lukin's *Ščepetil'nik* parades a succession of *petits-maîtres* and "giddy-pates" representing various aspects of society in St.-Petersburg during a public masquerade. The two peasants Lukin introduces did not appear in the original from which he adapted his own play. Fonvizin's *Brigadir* went a good deal further than any of Lukin's plays, in that the appearance, the ideas, the conduct and even the phraseology of the Brigadir, his wife and son, the Sovetnik and his wife, were all recognisably Russian. No other writer ventured as far as Fonvizin in portraying Russian characters, and he himself adhered − in both

[3] Bertha Malnick, "The theory and practice of Russian drama in the early 19th century", *Slavonic and East European Review*, 34 (1955), p. 16.
[4] John Dryden, *op. cit.*, p. 34.

*Brigadir* and *Nedorosl'* – to a principle that was generally observed throughout the first few decades of the Russian theatre. This was that Russian traits were bestowed most generously upon negative or low characters. The unsuccessful and foolish suitors, the bad-tempered or silly parents, the witty valets and maidservants, the peasants – these are the characters who bear Russian names, display Russian manners, wear Russian dress or use Russian dialect and proverbs. The hero and heroine, on the other hand, often have a few superficially Russian traits – some heroes are army or navy officers, or the heroines are said to have been educated at the Smolnyj Institute – but the majority remain very close to the insipid prototypes of French comedy.

The principle was observed well into the early nineteenth century. In the comedies of Šaxovskoj and Zagoskin, for instance, the frenchified dandies and the coquettes, the bad poets, the servants and the elderly relatives are recognisably Russian. The hero and heroine, for all their patriotic speeches and virtuous behaviour, continued to resemble the lovers in the French plays.

## II

### Speaking Names and Conventional Names

A device often used by playwrights to help an audience recognize personages and to identify their function in a play was the speaking name. Characters were given names deriving from their dominant vice or "humour". Roman playwrights had used the device, and it reappeared in French comedy of the seventeenth century, and in English comedy from Ben Jonson to the Restoration. Lukin adopted the device by deriving a speaking name from a Russian word, usually an adjective. This was part of his way of transposing foreign originals to Russian soil: as we saw in chapter I, he was always critical of Sumarokov's foreign names.

The speaking name usually denoted a ruling fault or vice, but it could also indicate a character's prevailing virtue. Characters whose function was to exhort virtue were christened Dobroserdov, Dobron-ravov, Dobromylsov or Zdravomyslov: other bore names deriving from *pravda* (Pravdin, Pravodum), *milyj* (Milovid, Milon, Premil, Milena), *čest'* (Česton, Čestona, Čestin, Čestan) or *razum* (Blagorazumov).

Names signalising vices were still more ingenious and telling: misers are called Čužexvat or Skrjagin: pedants Kutejkin or Inkvartus: third-rate poets and plagiarists Rifmokrad or Rifmoxvat: fops Verxolet, Vetron, Fifljufjuškov: the snob Važnikov: drunkards Kapel'kin or Bul'bul'kin. Characters ruled by folly include Puston, Glupon, Pustorečin, Vetrodumov, Slabodum, Oglupov, Prostodum, Prostakov, Vzdorova and Legkomysla. Cheats and hypocrites were Licemerov, Jadon, Zmejad, Podlecovskij, Zlorad.

A character in Klušin's *Alximist* went as far as to explain to the audience how his speaking name had been invented: he is a Russian artist who has taken to drink because of the indifference of contemporary society: "My surname . . . is formed of two words, a noun and an epithet – and although my name should be Gorep'janov, I have christened myself Sgorep'janov."

A further variation on the speaking name was that it could be used to denote a profession: doctors are Lansetin or Smertodav: a tutor is Cyfirkin.[5]

By the 1790s, the speaking name was often used with a Russian first name and patronymic, and the continued use of the device in the early 1800s by Šaxovskoj and in 1823 by Griboedov demonstrate the close connection seen to exist between the device and the traditions of satirical comedy. The *haute comédie* of the 1810s rarely used it: only one of Xmel'nickij's many comedies introduces characters with speaking names.

As a rule, conventional names were preferred for heroines, usually with a Slavonic rather than French flavour. The names Prelesta, Milena, Prjata or Sofia were especially popular, even though Karamzin complained in 1791 that in comedy "people should not only behave but also be named as they are in life".[6] But such names persist through this period, and are indeed a kind of speaking name themselves. Valets and maid-servants were also given names drawn from a small fund of names considered appropriate to their station in life: they are called Andrej, Prolaz, Trofim, Mavra, Daša, Maša or Saša. Knjažnin's *Čudaki* suggests the importance of names in comedy: the hero of the play is advised to ingratiate himself with the foolish philosopher Lentjagin by calling himself Semeon – a name invariably bestowed on servants in Russian comedy. But he indignantly refuses to do anything of the sort,

[5] The "cyfirnye" schools were opened by Peter I in 1714, cf. K. V. Pigarev, *Tvorčestvo Fonvizina* (Moscow, 1954), p. 174.

[6] Quoted by I. A. Krjažimskaja, "Iz istorii teatral'noj kritiki konca XVIII -- načala XIX veka", in Akademija nauk S.S.S.R., *XVIII vek*, IV (Moscow-Leningrad, 1959), p. 214.

even if adopting such a low name might help him win the heroine's hand.

## III

### *The "Raisonneurs"*

The classification of personages in comedy had become rigidly fixed, even fossilised, on the French stage by the end of the seventeenth century. Molière's *l'Avare* and *Le Misanthrope* were followed by Regnard's *Le Joueur* (1696) and *Le Distrait* (1697). The plays' titles act as signals to the audience, indicating both the theme that will be dealt with and the central character. The lovers in such plays are merely "passive objects round whom the intrigue revolves",[7] and are assisted by servants who amuse themselves and the audience at the expense of the miser, the misanthrope, the gamester or the absent-minded man, as the case may be. In addition to these figures, Regnard's comedies had introduced a still more important character, absent from the comedies of Molière, but who was to come to the forefront in the Russian theatre. He was the "raisonneur", whose prime function was to voice the author's own views on a wide range of subjects, from duty and honour, to patriotic obligations, service to the State and good manners.

The appearance and development of the raisonneur's role in satirical comedy naturally ran parallel to the increase in the moralising element in such plays. As a literary type, he derives partly from the moralising narrator of the *Tatler* and *Spectator* essays by Addison and Steele, which enjoyed a very great popularity throughout Europe. The essays were translated into French in 1714, and into Russian in 1725.[8]

In the 1750s, Sumarokov had been content to satirise foibles and absurdities without enforcing his satire by the addition of a "raisonneur". In this respect he followed Molière. An early example of the species appears in Lukin's *Ščepetil'nik,* where the toy-shop vendor himself points out and derides the follies of his customers. The army officer Čistoserdov, who complements the remarks of the toy-shop vendor, occasionally expands them still further. In this respect, Čistoserdov plays the part of the second "raisonneur", a well-defined type

---

[7]  Jean Hankiss, *P. N. Destouches* (Debrecen, 1918), p. 280.
[8]  A. Veselovskij, *Zapadnoe vlijanie v novoj russkoj literature,* 2nd ed. (Moscow, 1896), p. 104.

in moralising comedy, whose function it was to support the first "raisonneur" against the more numerous fools and vicious personages.

The "raisonneurs' come into their own in the comedies of Fonvizin, of which Belinskij said: "The characters . . . are either fools or intelligent people, the former being caricatures, the latter 'raisonneurs' ". [9] In *Brigadir*, the role of the "raisonneur" is taken by Dobroljubov, who is at the same time the hero of the love intrigue, and as such is a personage of secondary importance in the play. The early version of *Nedorosl'* also contains one "raisonneur" only, though in the final version of 1782, Fonvizin was so anxious to convey the points he wished to make that he introduced two, as Lukin had done twenty years earlier. Both Starodum and Pravdin contribute to the play's intrigue and it is they who bring about the sequestration of Prostakova's estate, an incident which provides the denouement. But to Fonvizin these two personages were more useful as a means for propagating his own ideas on education, virtue, the duty of the monarchy and gentry, and rules of good conduct. His contemporaries recognized this, and somewhat later Vjazemskij declared: "It is often the author himself who speaks in the comedies of Fonvizin." [10] To emphasise the impression caused by the moralising of Starodum and Pravdin, Fonvizin skilfully differentiated their views on such general subjects as the purpose of enlightenment, though their views of subjects of more immediate relevance to the audience – virtue, honour, good sense – are identical. Their views on the monarchy are also differentiated, since Starodum – as his speaking name indicates – thinks more of the past than of the present.

Starodum's moralising speeches make up some 20 per cent of the total dialogue of *Nedorosl'*, and he was one of the most celebrated and popular of all the eighteenth-century "raisonneurs". His speeches are often abbreviated in present-day productions, but it was these speeches which contributed to the success of the play when first performed. Karamzin said of this aspect of the play that "the comic scenes were successful, but the main attention of the public was upon the serious scenes" of moralising.[11] In Court circles, however, the character Starodum – with his traditional views on the virtues and qualities of a

---

[9] Quoted in A. M. Gordin, ed., *A. S. Griboedov v russkoj kritike* (Moscow, 1958), p. 171.
[10] P. A. Vjazemskij, *Polnoe sobranie sočinenij*, ed. by S. D. Šeremetev, V (St.-Petersburg, 1880), p. 132.
[11] B. N. Vsevolodskij-Gerngross, *Russkij teatr vtoroj poloviny XVIII veka* (Moscow, 1960), p. 223.

genuinely enlightened monarch and court – was less popular, and was ridiculed in epigrams.[12]

Fonvizin's "raisonneurs" are more interesting than his colourless hero Milon, and this shift of interest from hero to "raisonneur" was typical of Russian comedy in this period. Two "raisonneurs" appear in Kop'ev's *Obraščennyj mizantrop*, in the figures of the Prince and his friend Dostojnov. Kop'ev failed to differentiate between these two as skilfully as Fonvizin distinguished between Starodum and Pravdin, so that Dostojnov does little more than echo the Prince, or ask leading questions so that the latter can expatiate at still greater length on topics which interested the author.

Other "raisonneurs" who express views held by their authors include Česton, the hero's father in Knjažnin's *Xvastun,* who advises his son on the importance of good conduct in the acquisition of genuine nobility. Starovek in Klušin's *Smex i gore* praises the advantages of the past; while the Graf in Kropotov's *Fomuška* discusses in detail the virtues of various systems of education.

The "raisonneur" underwent an eclipse on the Russian stage in the 1790s. No doubt audiences were growing more sophisticated and had less taste for direct moralising; but this was also the period immediately following the French Revolution, when writers for the most part preferred not to voice opinions on significant matters. In any case, both Krylov and Knjažnin were less directly concerned with moralising than their predecessors, and tended to offer didacticism in less obvious ways. Criticising the comedy *Smex i gore* in 1791, Krylov pointed out the artificiality of the "raisonneur", and deliberately omitted the species from his own *Modnaja lavka* and *Urok dočkam*. The "raisonneurs" in the comedies of Šaxovskoj and Zagoskin play significant parts in the intrigue in addition to voicing the opinions of their authors. Even so, Xolmskij and his like are clearly related to their eighteenth-century prototypes, as Puškin discerned when he called Xolmskij a "soporific sermoniser and inflated pedant",[13] – a phrase that might have been used of almost any of the earlier "raisonneurs". Griboedov's Čackij fulfils some of the functions of a "raisonneur", but "what a distance there is between the declamations of a Starodum, and the caustic invective of Čackij"![14]

[12]   B. N. Aseev, *Russkij dramatičeskij teatr XVII-XVIII vv.* (Moscow, 1958), pp. 261-2, quoting P. Arapov, *Letopis' russkogo teatra* (St.-Petersburg, 1861), p. 110.
[13]   *Puškin v teatre* (Moscow, 1953), p. 304.
[14]   Jules Patouillet, *Le Théâtre de mœurs russe* (Paris, 1912), p. 59.

But the decline steadily continued. The "raisonneur" had no place in "blagorodnaja komedija", and the popularity of these plays no doubt contributed to O. M. Somov's comment in 1825 that "raisonneurs" were the "most tedious and stodgy personages in comedy".[15]

## IV

### Hero and Heroine

The hero and heroine round whom the intrigues of Russian comedy revolves resemble their French counterparts who also suffer most, but do the least. They are sympathetically presented by playwrights, but their love intrigue is little more than a pretext for erecting a series of comic complications involving other characters. The hero and heroine are never the central characters in Russian comedy – until Sofia and Čackij emerge in *Gore ot uma*.

This method of treating the lovers in comedy was that practised by the French playwrights of the late seventeenth century. In Molière's plays, the lovers often seem like little more than padding. But in the 1730s, playwrights were beginning to turn their attention to love as well as satire. At this time, Marivaux was writing his "études de métaphysique amoureuse",[16] although "marivaudage", with its studies of inner conflict, analysis of sentiment and refined language did not exert a marked influence on contemporary or later Russian comedy. Lukin translated several of Marivaux's plays, including *La (Seconde) surprise d'amour* (1727). However, his understanding of the original can be estimated by his mistranslation of the title, which refers to a second play with the title *La surprise d'amour*: Lukin renders the title as *Vtorično vkravšajsja ljubov'* (1765).[17] But the lovers in Russian comedy never struggle against their own feelings, nor do Russian playwrights demonstrate any of Marivaux's interest in psychological states of mind.

Naturally, the heroes of comedy are young men of virtue and honour. They speak in elevated and refined diction, even when they are peasants (as in the comic opera libretti of Knjažnin and others). Valerij, the hero of Sumarokov's *Opekun* ("The Guardian", 1766) is a typical hero: he

---

[15]  A. M. Gordin, ed., *A. S. Griboedov v russkoj kritike* (Moscow, 1958), p. 20.
[16]  G. Lanson, *Nivelle de la Chaussée*, 2nd ed. (Paris, 1903), p. 36.
[17]  K. N. McKee, *The Theater of Marivaux* (New York, 1958), p. 99.

contrasts himself for the audience's benefit with the miserly and snob-
bish Čužexvat: "I follow no fashions, only sincere and wholesome good
sense, natural simplicity and elevated taste – a fashion that will never
change" (sc. 10). The hero of *Brigadir* assures the heroine: "Our love
is based on honourable intentions", in contrast to the conduct of other
personages in the play, who pay court to one another's wives, and
whose behaviour is "ludicrous, superficial and shameful" (I, 5).
Pravdin, the "reformed misanthrope" in Kop'ev's play of 1794, declares he has been forced by "wounded sensibility, disappointed hopes
and extreme poverty" to seek solitude in the countryside, where he
can "avoid contact with persons who stifle virtue with glittering
baubles" (V, 1).

For all their protestations, however, the heroes tend to behave in a
singularly unheroic manner when they encounter obstacles in their
courtship of the heroines. More often than not, they react to the news
that a rival has (temporarily) outwitted them by giving way to instant
despair in a manner clearly deriving from the "comédie larmoyante",
a genre which contaminated comedy proper throughout the eighteenth
century, and which is considered in more detail in Chapter III. Examples of such heroes include Liubim, in Nikolev's comic opera *Rozana
i Ljubim* who swoons away upon seeing Rozana kidnapped by the
"barin", and is absent for the rest of the play, reappearing only in the
finale of the last act, when the intrigue has been resolved and nothing
remains but for Ljubim to claim the hand of Rozana. Fonvizin's Milon
utters a cry of anguish at the mere thought of his sweetheart Sofia in
the hands of "self-seekers" such as the Prostakov family (*Ned.*, II, 1).
When Pol'evkt hears that the heroine Evfimija is being sought in
marriage by other suitors, he gives way to instant dejection, though
Evfimija herself assures him all will be well, and the other suitors are
ludicrous boobies (Čulkov's *Kak xočeš, nazovi,* "Call It What You
Will", 1783). A rumour that Sofia may be wedded to someone else is
enough to drive Prjamikov to a state of "anguish" (*Jab.*, 1, 2), Milon
protests he "would sooner lose my life than your hand in marriage"
(*Prokazniki*, I, 12), while Ostromyslov calls on the Deity to observe
that his "mind is reeling ... I have a roaring in my ears ... I am all
in disorder ..." because he is too poor to pay court to the heroine of
*Fomuška* (IV, 1).

However, the "comédie larmoyante" was not exclusively responsible
for the sentimentality of these heroes: the historian Ključevskij pointed
out that "the Russian gentleman (*'dvorjanin'*) was never so impression-

able, so susceptible, never gave way to his enthusiasm nor wept so promptly as during the reign of Catherine".[18]

Playwrights were quick to seize upon the fashionable sensibility of these heroes and heroines for purposes of satire and parody. The sentimental heroes and heroines of popular fiction were ridiculed by Knjažnin and Krylov, and later by Šaxovskoi and Zagoskin. It was thus but a step from the "man of feeling" Zamir in *Xvastun*, whose sentimental speeches are meant seriously, to the hero of *Čudaki*, whose sensibility is mocked and parodied. Here Prijat is so overcome by his feelings that he cannot even speak to the heroine without the encouragement of his valet. Šaxovskoj depicts the "new Sterne" who yearns to marry a "simple village maiden", and holds up his exaggerated sensibility to ridicule (*Novyj Stern*, 1804).

Whether the hero and heroine are depicted as sensitive beings or creatures of parody, their roles in comedy remains secondary. Indeed, the love intrigue in a number of plays is treated in a manner that borders on the perfunctory; the hero of *Smex i gore* declares in the first act that he loves and hopes to marry the heroine, but once this declaration has been made, the matter is not referred to again, and the play is entirely concerned with ridiculing the foolish Mrs Vzdorova. Krylov was so unconcerned with the heroine in his *Prokazniki* that she is sometimes referred to as the daughter of Rifmokrad, and elsewhere as his niece. Knjažnin introduces the hero of the very long 5-act *Čudaki* in only five brief scenes. The love of Prjamikov for the heroine of *Jabeda* is briefly mentioned in Act I, after which Kapnist devotes his attention exclusively to satirising Krivosudov and his corrupt officials.

This perfunctory treatment of hero and heroine affects the characterisation of these personages. Since the playwrights were primarily concerned with obtaining immediate recognition for each character introduced, methods had to be found for "placing" the heroes. In addition to the speaking names used for this purpose, writers often provided their heroes with an easily recognisable social or other rank. Thus a number of heroes in comedies are Army or Naval officers, whose service to the State constituted an essential part of their virtue. It was enough for the playwrights' purpose to state that the hero was a soldier or sailor (of officer rank), and that he was virtuous: there was no need to waste time proving it. Hence military life was regarded as an appropriate career for stage heroes throughout the period – from Lukin's

[18] V. O. Ključevskij, *Kurs russkoj istorii*, 5 (Moscow, 1937), p. 214.

Army officer and reformed gambler in *Mot* (1765) to Šaxovskoj's young men recently returned from the Napoleonic campaigns in *Urok koketkam* and other plays. During Catherine's reign, however, the military and naval heroes rarely give voice to patriotic utterances, and at least one writer made his naval lieutenant hero criticise Russia by implication. This was Kop'ev's Ostromyslov, whose description of foreign countries he has visited include an oblique reference to a "state without laws", which the audience may have interpreted as referring to Russia. It was not until after 1815 that patriotic speeches became an essential part of every hero's role, and were attributes as admirable as his virtue and sensibility. Thus Pronskij asserts that his bravery on the battlefield was "simply following the example of the immortal glory of our nation" (*Urok koketkam*), and Zagoskin's Vladimirov utters a tirade in praise of Russia to offset the sneers of the 'umnik" Bleskin that "our dear homeland has no Louvre, no Palais Royal and no Tuileries" (*Bog.*, III, 3).

The relations between hero and heroine are based on mutual respect rather than on romantic feelings. The heroes are attracted to the heroines because of the "innocence" of the latter. Even the misanthrope Pravdin, who has quit society because of its falsity, falls in love with Ljubov because of her "childish innocence", and describes her as "a pure-hearted soul, full of sensibility" (*Obr. miz.*, V, 1). The army officer Izved, who falls in love with Paša by seeing her for a moment at a window, praises her "sweet innocence", and contrasts her with "women educated in the great world, whom everyone knows" (*Sbit.*, I, 1).

As the playwrights were not concerned with dramatising the relations between hero and heroine, it was necessary to find some external obstacle to the smooth course of the love intrigue. This obstacle was most easily provided by the parents or guardian of the hero or heroine – sometimes of both. Thus the parents and guardians in Russian comedy almost invariably attempt to force an unsuitable, disagreeable husband upon their daughter or ward, even though she is in love with the hero. The Sovetnik's daughter Sofia, who loves Dobroljubov and is loved by him, is to "marry a man who has been to Paris", though she knows he is a fool and says so, in the first scene of *Brigadir*. Xristina is to be forced to marry the "silliest" of her suitors, because her father has chosen him (*Nevesta nevidimka,* "The Invisible Lady", 1772). Sometimes the heroine makes an attempt to rebel against her parents' wishes: Rozana declares: "I will remain a spinster, which (sighing) I do not at all want to do", rather than marry the man of her father's choice (*Rozana i Ljubim*, I, 3). Similarly Xavronja seeks to rebel against her father's choice of suitor, the retired official Krjučkodej (*SPb. Gost. dvor*, 1791). Sofia becomes a pawn in the schemes of Mrs. Prostakova, who seeks to marry her off to Mitrofan, the ignorant "minor" of *Nedorosl'*, and Malan'ja is to be married to the foolish "granny's boy", Fomuška, because her father wishes it so. But Malan'ja loves Ostromyslov and declares "better drown than marry Foma" (IV, 7). The heroine of *Jabeda*, although she does not venture to rebel, complains that she "gets no peace, even in sleep", from the official Pravolov, whose courtship is supported by her father.

If the heroine is an orphan, she is provided with a guardian who has designs upon her person or her property. Čužexvat wishes to marry his ward Sostrata to a "fool" so that he may retain control of her fortune for himself (*Opekun*). The miser of Knjažnin's *Skupoi* ("The Miser", 1788) attempts to do the same, while the rich but foolish merchant Boldyrev has brought up his ward Paša for the sole purpose of marrying her himself (*Sbit.*).

Despite the tyranny exercised over heroines by their parents and guardians, they never rebel completely, and indeed will frequently declare their filial devotion to the preposterous monsters set up as parents in Russian comedy. Despite her sufferings, Ljubov vows she "will not do anything against the will of my parents" (*Obr. miz.*, 1, 3) and Prjata urges her lover Milon to "obey your uncle, even though he wishes to separate us" (*Prok.*, I, 11). The peasant girl Anjuta tells Matvej, who loves her: "I will die without you, but shall never be your wife against the wishes of my parents" (*Bobyl'*, III, 3). Xristina declares "my mother's will is law to me" although her mother, the absurd Mrs. Vorčalkina, is seeking to marry her to a man Xristina heartily despises. This filial devotion persists throughout the period, and as late as 1819 Sofia agrees to marry the foolish Pososkov, whose head has been turned by novel-reading, merely "because my aunt wants me to" (in Zagoskin's *Roman na bol'šoj doroge*).

Clearly, these personages did not interest the playwrights greatly, and the parts provided by such roles were never of much consequence. Not until *Gore ot uma* did the hero and heroine come to the forefront in comedy, and appear as interesting characters in their own right. Sofia and Čackij were regarded by contemporaries as "startingly unconventional" characters.[19] Here, for the first time in Russian comedy,

[19] Bertha Malnick, "The Theory and practice of Russian drama in the early nineteenth century", *Slavonic and East European Review*, 34 (1955), p. 14.

the hero and heroine become the central figures in a play, standing out against a background of satirical portraits and types. The relationship between them has been described as "in striking disharmony among ... the practically indistinguishable young lovers of Russian comedy",[20] and this was no doubt one of the reasons why these two roles were regarded by actors as "ungrateful" as late as 1910.[21]

However, the eighteenth-century playwrights were able to provide parts containing more opportunities for the traditional style of comedy acting, in roles for foolish women. Ridiculous, often elderly women in love appear in a number of comedies produced during Catherine's reign. Catherine herself found some of these caricatures offensive,[22] but such personages were a perennial figure of fun on the European stage, and were to be epitomised in the comic operas of W. S. Gilbert. Examples included the heroine's elderly aunt, who falls in love with the reformed gambler in Lukin's *Mot,* though he is in love with the heroine. Kušin's Vetxokrasova, who begs the alchemist to sell her an elixir of love to "repair my complexion damaged by love and illness" was another.

Not all the foolish women in Russian comedy are figures of fun. Fonvizin's portrayal of the species in both his plays is one of the means by which he illustrated his superior gift for characterisation over those of his contemporaries. He succeeds in rendering the ignorant Brigadir's wife as an absurd yet at the same time pathetic woman, suffering at the hands of her coarse husband (IV, 2). Prostakova's fate resembles that which comes upon overfond mothers in sentimental drama, when she is spurned by her son in the finale of *Nedorosl'.* Here, Prostakova is a figure in whom are concealed "all the ferocious passions necessary for tragic presentations. ... As Tartuffe stands mid-way between tragedy and comedy, so does Prostakova".[23]

But Fonvizin's successors were content to revert to the caricatures of foolish women already familiar in the plays of Sumarokov and Lukin. As well as being unsuitably in love, these women often personify follies and foibles of contemporary society, and this is made clear in their speaking names. Čvankina, whose main foible is pride, is a "rich widow newly arrived in St.-Petersburg", who schemes to marry her daughter to the pretended "Graf" Verxolet (*Xvastun*). Mrs.

[20]  *Ibid.,* p. 14.
[21]  A. M. Gordin, *op. cit.,* p. 290.
[22]  See Chapter I.
[23]  P. A. Vjazemskij, *op. cit.,* p. 136.

Lentjagina, married to the indolent "philosopher" Lentjagin, boasts of her husband's ancestry and his knowledge of French, only to be exposed for her pains in front of the impoverished fop Vetromax (*Čudaki*). Knjažnin ridicules all the heroine's female relatives – mother, aunt and grandmother – in his *Bešennaya sem'ja* ("A Frenzied Family", 1786), as they each "fall in love" with the hero Postan and believe he is in love with each of them. Krylov's Novomodovaja is depicted reading a list of her "lovers" and the presents they have given her in *Sočinitel' v prixožei*, though the "lovers" are no doubt as harmless as those listed by Dickens' silly Lady Tippins.[24]

## Coquettes and Blue-Stockings

From the "flirt" Novomodovaja to the "grandes coquettes" of French comedy was not far. But the coquettes who appear in the Russian comedies of the early nineteenth-century have their counterparts in the *vetropraxi* or "giddy-pates" of the plays of Lukin and his contemporaries. Two such ladies, Nimfodora and Marem'jana visit the toy-shop vendor to purchase extravagant trifles and mock the moralising with which he castigates them (*Ščepetil'nik*). Elagin portrays a *Nakazannaja vetropražka* ("A Giddy-Pate Punished", 1767), surrounded by an entourage of grafs and courtiers, all of whom despise Russia and the Russian language, deride "Lomonosov and Feofan" (Prokopovich) and "glory in their ignorance". Catherine's Olympiada, who takes four hours every day to complete her toilette (*Vorč.*), is a predecessor of the coquette Leleva, portrayed in detail by Šaxovskoj forty years later in *Urok koketkam*.

Leleva epitomises the "grandes coquettes" of Russian comedy. As the title shows, she is the central character of the play, and her part is longer and more theatrically rewarding than that of the insipid heroine. Leleva "lies in bed all day, which is not surprising since she is at balls all night long, with her spine and her shoulders bare . . .". She has come to Lipec Spa "to cure her nerves". Her arrival has caused all the other ladies at the Spa to "take to their beds", or "go home, dragging their husbands and brothers with them". In addition to being a coquette, Leleva has much in common with the fashionable "umnik" Ol'gin. She expresses her dislike of St.-Petersburg "with its insufferable etiquette, dinner parties, stuffy theatres . . . where gossip spares neither friends nor relatives" (II, 5). She makes great play at being discovered

[24]  Charles Dickens, *Our Mutual Friend*.

by her admirers reading Lévêque's *History of Russia* (in French),
though her maid informs the audience in an aside that this is merely a
device to draw attention to her "learning" (III, 7). By endowing Leleva
with this pretended love for serious literature, Šaxovskoj associates her
with the blue-stockings, another group of women frequently satirised
in the French antiphilosopher comedies and in the Russian theatre.
Krylov had provided an early example in his female poetess Taratora
(*Prokazniki*), but the type was depicted in greatest detail by Zagoskin.
His widow Radugina is preoccupied with literary composition and the
publication of a journal, as well as holding a "bureau d'esprit" for
third-rate literary hacks (*Večernika učenyx*).

When the coquettes are not blue-stockings, they are affected with
sensibility, often through reading sentimental novels and poetry. Like
the "giddy-pates" of the 1760s and 1770s, these ladies are never the
heroine, but may be her mother or aunt. It is the heroine's mother
Mrs. Vspyškin who plans a "sentimental breakfast" and hopes "a
sweet nightingale will embellish our breakfast with its harmonies ..."
(*Pirog*, sc. 7). Her husband blames her sentimentality on "novel reading,
which has driven her out of her senses". Similarly, it is the hero's aunt
in Šaxovskoj's contribution to *Svoja sem'ja* ("One's own Family",
1818) who is convinced from her reading of novels that "town society
is depraved", and will have made the heroine into a woman "unable
to be sympathetic". The artful heroine Nataša gains this lady's favours
by pretending the love "feelings, sentimentality and novel-reading", and
admiring the most celebrated sentimental novel of the day, Karamzin's
*Bednaja Liza* ("Poor Liza"). The change in taste from sentimental
to "Gothick" fiction is illustrated in Zagoskin's Mrs. Landyščva, who
voices her "raptures over wild landscapes" and her fondness for "The
Mysteries of Udolpho" and "The Abbey of St. Clare", two of Mrs.
Radcliffe's popular novels.


V

*Unsuccessful Suitors*


A character who almost invariably played a larger part in comedies
than either hero or heroine was the latter's unsuccessful suitor. This
personage gave the playwrights ample opportunity to develope the
essential moralising purpose of their plays – mocking vices and foibles,

and thereby hoping to correct them. The unsuccessful suitors depicted in eighteenth- and early nineteenth-century comedies provide examples of all the faults and follies which playwrights observed in contemporary society. These personages display extravagance, Gallomania, conceit – as well as the cowardice, ignorance and corruption of badly-educated gentry and officials; and by contrast, the heroes appear all the more admirable, and the heroines emphasize their own virtue and good sense by despising and ridiculing them.

The commonest fault to afflict the unsuccessful suitors of comedy between 1765 and the 1780s is Gallomania. Characters exhibiting this fault are closely related to the "petits-maîtres" of French society, whom Voltaire described as "la jeunesse impertinente et mal élevée", and who were satirised in such plays as Marivaux' *Le Petit-Maître corrigé* (1734).[25] Ivan in Fonvizin's *Brigadir* displays all the characteristic traits of the Russian "petit-maître", from his contempt for Russia, the Russian language and his own family, to his use of the fashionable Franco-Russian jargon. Knjažnin provides another example in Vetro-max, who "speaks Russian only with footmen, coachmen and other common people, when there is no need to think" (*Čud.*, II, 2). The species survives into the 1820s: Bleskin, who has lived two years in Paris, is described as a "half-French petit-maître" in Zagoskin's *Bogatonov*, and he follows in the footsteps of his predecessors by failing to win the hand of the heroine. By this time, however, the traits of the Russian "petits-maîtres" had become more closely associated with the fashionable "umniki" ridiculed by Šaxovskoj.[26]

Other unsuccessful suitors, each with his characteristic fault or folly often denoted by a speaking name, included Vestoliub, in whom "curiosity has become a detestable vice" (*Nevesta nev.*, sc. 1), and Pravolov, the "wicked chicaner" of *Jabeda,* whose courtship of the heroine overshadows that of the virtuous hero of the play. But neither Catherine nor Kapnist, in these two plays, made much attempt to contrast the unsuccessful suitor and the hero, except by implication. This method was generally adopted during the eighteenth-century, however. Fonvizin contrasts the foolish Ivan of *Brigadir* with the hero Dobroliubov merely by implication, since these two personages do not come into conflict and indeed rarely address one another. Ivan goes so far as to persuade the Sovetnitsa to leave Sofia alone with Do-broljubov (I, 4). In the same way, Milon and his rival Mitrofan in

[25] K. N. McKee, *op. cit.*, p. 175.
[26] See Chapter I.

*Nedorosl'* never address one another, and almost the same situation prevails in *Fomuška*; here Ostromyslov and his rival Fomuška hold a brief conversation which is intended to display the former's intelligence and the latter's stupidity, but there is no conflict between them, and each seems indifferent to the fact that the other is his rival for the hand of Malan'ja.

Šaxovskoj saw the theatrical possibilities inherent in this rivalry, and exploited it in several of his plays. The confirmed liar Zarnitskij is "taught a lesson" by the hero Mezeckij, who also warns him that "he who lies is never believed again" (*Ne ljubo – ne slušai*, "Don't Listen If You Don't Want To", 1818), Zagoskin points the contrast between his hero Izborskij and the malicious "umnik" in *Komedija protiv komedii* by endowing the latter with an absurd name (Tjulipan) and a passion for playing cards, which Izborskij despises. Izborskij comes into direct conflict with Tjulipan when the "umnik" patronises the heroine Sofia, believing her penniless (I, 8).

But the unsuccessful suitors on the Russian stage after 1815 are no longer the grotesque personifications of vices or foibles who peopled the eighteenth-century stage. Griboedov's portrayal of Molčalin in *Gore ot uma* carries the development of this type a good deal further. Although Molčalin is a hypocrite and time-server, he has succeeded in inducing the heroine to fall in love with him. Were it not for his speaking name, the audience might take Molčalin for the hero when the play starts and he is discovered in Sofia's room, after spending the night there, reading. The rivalry between Čackij and Molčalin gives the play its structural centre; and, to complete the reversal of their roles, it is Molčalin who defeats Čackij and brings about his flight, when Čackij realises that Sofia prefers his rival.


# VI

## *Parents*

Although the hero and heroine of Russian comedy want nothing better than to marry, marriage is presented as a disagreeable state. Husbands are over-bearing, tyrannous, bad-tempered, eccentric, jealous, unfaithful, domineering and fault-finding. They brow-beat, quarrel with and even strike their wives. The only exceptions to this rule occur when it is the wife who is over-bearing, tyrannical, quarrelsome and bad-tempered, and the husband who is nagged, scolded and struck by his wife. Sumarokov's *Ssora u muža* (1750) was a prototype for this husband-wife relationship, and the play includes nearly all the elements of unhappy married life which later playwrights exploited so frequently. In this play, Orint and his wife support rival suitors for the hand of their daughter Delamida, and during the course of the slight intrigue which follows, Orint's wife puts him to flight on two separate occasions (scenes 10 and 24), though he begs the servant Klimar to protect him.

Just as the French theatre abounded in tyrannical parents who opposed the romantic inclinations of their children, so the Russian husbands and wives favour and support unsuccessful suitors and reject the virtuous hero. Sometimes two suitors will be supported by husband and wife respectively, a situation Sumarokov used in *Ssora* and which recurs in such plays and comic opera libretti as Nikolev's *Mel'nik-koldun* ("The Miller-Magician", 1772), Čulkov's *Kak xočeš, nazovi* (1783) and Catherine's *Razstroennaja sem'ja* (1786), and elsewhere. This situation enabled playwrights to introduce elements of farce into their comedies, since the disagreements which result between husband and wife provide opportunities for displays of bad temper, quarrels and brawls.

The relations generally prevailing between husband and wife in Russian comedy before 1800 are best illustrated in Fonvizin's *Brigadir* and *Nedorosl'*. Both the husbands in *Brigadir* despise their own wives, and attempt to pay court to each other's. The Brigadir's views on marriage make him "forbid friend or enemy to get married" (IV, 2), a remark which is the more telling since it immediately follows a scene in which the hero and heroine expatiate on the delights of matrimony. The Brigadir's son Ivan tells his mother: "It is enough to see you and father together to acquire a total aversion to marriage" (V, 1). Although married to the Sovetnik, the Sovetnica flirts outrageously with Ivan, and describes her husband as "a fool" (V, 2). In *Nedorosl'*, the relations between Mr. and Mrs. Prostakova are the reverse of those between the Brigadir and his wife; here it is the wife who makes her husband "stutter with timidity" in her presence (I, 3), and is described by Pravdin as a "vile-tempered fury", whose "infernal conduct makes a misery of the entire household" (II, 1).

Sometimes the role of the "père comique" is replaced by that of the "père noble", who is also a "raisonneur". The hero's father Česton in *Xvastun* is a "councillor of the local administration", who encourages his son and provides him with sensible advice on how to win the

heroine's hand, as well as discoursing to him on morality and virtue
(III, 1). Česton even interferes in the play's intrigue, and warns the
foolish Mrs. Čvankina as to the true character of the "boaster" Verxolet. But Česton is an exception to the ludicruous or ignorant fathers
of Russian comedy, and no doubt owes much to the "père noble" of
sentimental drama.

By 1815, the fathers and mothers of the heroine have disappeared,
and their places taken by more distant relatives, usually an uncle or
aunt. Zagoskin never depicts a father or mother: in *Komedija protiv
komedii* it is the heroine's aunt, herself a coquette, who places obstacles
in the way of the hero's courtship. Šaxovskoj consistently avoided depicting fathers and mothers; Princess Xolmskaja is the heroine's aunt
(*Urok kok.*), and it is Radugin's uncle who comes to his rescue in
*Pustodomy*. Leleva's aunt contributes to the intrigue of *Kakadu*, and
Germont of Xmel'nickij's *Šalosti vljublennyx* ("Lovers' Follies", 1817)
is the heroine's uncle. Evidently a reaction had set in against the caricaturing of parents, so frequent in the eighteenth-century drama.
Famusov is one of the few fathers to be depicted in comedy during
the early 1800s. This consistent refusal to depict parents in an un-
favourable light may be in part the result of the need playwrights felt
for distinguishing between comedy proper and the "comédie larmoyante", in which fathers and mothers continued to appear.


## VI


### *Servants*


Servants always played an important part in comedy. Roman comedy
had depicted artful and ingenious slaves, the *commedia dell'arte* had
its witty and impertinent servants, the French theatre after Molière
abounded in valets and chambermaids, who often represented the voice
of down-to-earth common-sense and aided the triumph of virtue. The
astute and enterprising valets and servant girls of Russian comedy are
closely related to this tradition. The steady growth of their importance
on the stage in this period was connected with a change which occurred
in the constitution of the audiences. This change took place after the
introduction into the public theatres of the gallery in 1783. In this year
the Court and the public theatres in St.-Petersburg were finally sepa-
rated; the Hermitage theatre was always an integral part of the royal

apartments, and was henceforward mostly used for productions by the French company.

The opening of the theatres to the general public brought a new element into the audiences, which had hitherto been almost entirely composed of nobility and gentry. As soon as the lower classes began filling the galleries, playwrights learned to introduce into their plays characters aimed at pleasing this vociferous section of the audience. Such audiences naturally enjoyed seeing representatives of their own class on the stage, especially as the playwrights almost always endowed the servants and other "low people" with wit, ingenuity and even impertinence.

Like their French counterparts, the servants in Russian comedy are often responsible for the play's intrigue. They advise and assist their masters or mistresses to overcome obstacles by the use of native common-sense, deceit or trickery. Like the valets and chambermaids of French comedy, they are always primarily concerned with the problems and difficulties which beset their masters, rarely with their own. Their function in the plays was as clearly defined as the functions of all the other personages.

In addition to planning, devising, executing and supervising the deceptions practised on their masters' rivals or on the heroine's foolish suitors, the servants provided broad, often farcical humour and buffoonery, intended to please the pit and gallery. They often open the plays and prepare for the entrance of the hero, heroine or unsuccessful suitor by discussing them. They provide comments on the course of the action as it progresses, and often convey to the audience the moral lesson to be learned from the play, in the traditional "mot à la fin".

The servants share one trait with the secondary personages discussed in the section that follows. They are the most "Russian" characters in comedy. Unlike the gentlefolk from whose ranks heroes, heroines, raisonneurs, parents and unsuccessful suitors are drawn, the servants are serfs and untainted by foreign cosmopolitan influences or by faulty education. The servants most nearly reflect conditions actually prevailing in society at this time. Fonvizin showed serfs ill-treated by the inhuman Mrs. Prostakova, but few other playwrights ventured to depict conditions as dreadful as those prevailing in the Prostakov household. For the most part, domestic servants (though serfs) are on more agreeable terms with their masters and mistresses. A few servants complain of their lot in terms like those used by Dmitrij (*Obr. miz.*) and Mitrofan, the hero's valet (*Fom.*) who have to get up early to prepare tea for their masters. But such complaints were restricted to comic monologues or asides, and do not prevent the valets from taking an active part in their masters' courtships.

Although Catherine's comedies were not performed in the public theatres, she introduced valets and chambermaids who closely resemble the servants of other Russian comedy. They represent the triumph of good sense, are capable of judging fools and are always ready to help virtuous characters to triumph over folly or vice. Like servants in French comedy, they may even be domestic philosophers, able to furnish their masters and mistresses with practical lessons. The maid Mavra is Xristina's confidante in *O Vremja!*, was responsible for her education and advises her how best to win the affection of the hero (II, 1). Mavra also points the moral of the play in the final scene. The maid Praskov'ja does not hesitate to scold the indolent Olympiada for 'dressing with an eye to pleasing the fop' Firljufušov, she quotes Russian aphorisms ("he who chases many hares often fails to catch any") and is entrusted with the "mot à la fin" (*Vorč.*). Both the valet and the maid in *Nevesta nevidimka* have their "own language", in which they freely discuss their master and mistress, and they direct the intrigue by persuading Marem'jana that the fop Vestoljub is in love with her, thus enabling the heroine to wed the hero instead of Vestoljub, whom her parents preferred.

Other servants who direct the intrigues and bring about the denouement include Kirak in Sumarokov's *Ssora,* Kirjak in Čulkov's *Kak xočeš nazovi,* who deliberately gives the heroine's foolish suitors misleading advice so that both are driven from the house, and the heroine's maid Marina (*Fom.*), who takes the liberty of telling the hero that the bashful heroine loves him. Like many other domestic servants in comedy, Marina speaks out boldly in defence of her mistress and even reproaches the latter's father for forcing the girl to mary the ignorant Fomuška. The penniless noblemen Verxolet (*Xvastun*) relies throughout the play on the advice and assistance of his valet Polist, who helps him deceive the foolish Prostodum into believing that Verxolet can obtain for him the rank of Senator. Polist also disembarrasses his master of importunate creditors, and it is Polist who extricates Verxolet from an awkward situation by "feeding" him with lines (I, 5). Polist comments in several monologues on the progress of his master's trickeries, conspires with the heroine's maid, acts as chaperone when Verxolet pays court to the heroine, and even joins in the dialogue between them with his own comments and witticisms (IV, 3). Another servant whose master – like Oblomov – relies upon him for every detail of life is Bezrazsudov, whose valet declares "without me, he could not take a step" (Efim'jev's sentimental comedy *Prestupnik ot igry,* "A Criminal from Gaming", 1788).

Knjažin introduced another witty and enterprising valet into *Čudaki,* in the personage Prolaz; he comments in asides on the eccentric behaviour of the "philosopher" Lentjagin, persuades the heroine's maid to assist him in furthering the courtship of his master, and advises the hero on what to say when paying his addresses to the heroine. Prolaz also provides the play with its "mot à la fin".

The inter-dependence between servants and their masters or mistresses is illustrated by the parallel courtships which develop between hero and heroine on one hand, and valet and maid on the other. This parallelism occured also in French comedy: the maid in Destouches' *l'Obstacle imprévu* declared: "A servant girl always loves the valet of him who sighs for her mistress. This is the rule" (I, 6). However, the valet's courtship of the maid is kept subordinate to that of the hero and heroine, nor do valet and maid reach an understanding until the hero has overcome all the obstacles to his union with the heroine. In Plavil'ščikov's *Bobyl'* three such parallel courtships develop; that of hero and heroine Čestin and Evgenija, who are gentlefolk, of the valet and maid and also of two "low" peasants. The valet Polist refers to the convention when he informs the maid: "Today both the count and I are to be married" (I, 10). The valet Semeon in Krylov's *Urok dočkam* complains he cannot marry the maid Daša until his master has won the heroine. Similarly, the maid Daša in Krylov's *Pirog* only accepts the valet Vanka when her mistress has obtained permission to marry the hero.

Fonvizin reveals his originality once again in the way he dispenses with these conventional servants. There are no servants in *Brigadir,* and the serfs in the Prostakov household are "Russian" and individuals, which cannot be said of the average domestic servants in other comedies. Fonvizin's portrayal of the old nurse Eremejevna in *Nedorosl'* shows a serf who is devoted to the callous and ignorant Mitrofan. She declares: "I will die but will not let the child (Mitrofan) be hurt!" One of Mitrofan's three domestic tutors, Cyfirkin, is a poor but independent ex-soldier serf, who refuses to accept his wages "for nothing" (V, 6). Even the servant-girl who has "been in bed since this morning" with a fever, is not mentioned to provide an opportunity for deriding an idle servant, but to illustrate Prostakova's attitude towards her household. But this attitude towards servants in comedy was not shared by Fonvizin's contemporaries. Not until the 1790s did a few other writers attempted to give more individuality to the servants depicted in their plays. The maid Plutana in Krylov's *Prokazniki* (1788/9) was a precursor of these servants; she has "been abroad, speaks French as well as any giddy-pate", and "reads romances" (I, 13). However, her role in the intrigue is still that of the ingenious maid whose wit serves only to help the hero and heroine. The heroine's maid in *Jabeda* was "educated at the Smolnyj' Institute for well-born girls", as was the heroine of the play and her maid Mašinka, in *Obraščennyj mizantrop*. The last-named is described in the *dramatis personae* as a "dvorjanka", and is depicted seated in the presence of her mistress (I, 4). That it was unusual for a servant to do this is shown in Knjažnin's *Čudaki*; when Mrs. Lentjagina comes upon Prolaz seated – at the invitation of her husband – she bursts into tears and swoons away. But apart from these superficial attempts at individualising the servants in plays, they function like the others in the gallery of conventional stereotypes.

By the 1790s the conventional servants of comedy were beginning to weary audiences and critics. Complaints had already been voiced in the French theatre by Destouches, who declared: "The valets should stay in the ante-room. Our valets in comedy are always diverting, a certain proof that they are insipid. If the writer were to leave them in the ante-room, where they ought to be, the action would then take place between the leading personages, and be more interesting and powerful." [27] Destouches said this in 1757, but so strong was the convention favouring witty but "insipid" valets in comedy that he himself introduced two valets into his next play, *Le fils naturel*. In Russia, Plavil'ščikov complained in 1792 that playwrights often made servants "more entertaining" than the rest of the characters, and had them "say things to their masters no serf would ever dare to say". He added that servants in comedy were "the most diverting but least true-to-life characters".[28] This explains why many leading actors of the time often preferred to specialise in the parts of servants,[29] and also why a tendency now begins for the valet in comedy to play an increasingly less important role. None of the male characters in *Urok koketkam* has a valet, and Petruška, Famuzov's valet in *Gore ot uma* plays no part in the intrigue and only speaks once, in reply to his master.

[27] Felix Gaiffe, *Le Drame en France au XVIIIe siècle* (Paris, 1910), p. 386.
[28] Quoted in V. V. Kallaš and N. E. Efros, *op. cit.*, p. 339.
[29] *Ibid.*, p. 174.

Parallel with this tendency, however, the role of maidservants in comedy expands. Destouches approved of this when he said of the "soubrettes" of French comedy: "Let them remain on the stage until our education improves and mothers and fathers become the confidantes of their children instead of the maidservants".[30] In Russian comedy too it was the usefulness of their roles as confidantes which brought servant-girls to the forefront. Whereas the hero could be provided with a "friend" in whom to confide (Pronskij and Xolmskij of *Urok koketkam*), so the servant-girl or chambermaid provided an audience for the heroine's confidences.

Zagoskin was well aware of the conventional treatment meted out to servant-girls in comedy, and derided it in *Komedija protiv komedii*. Here the maid Daša declares she "longs to go to the play" (meaning *Urok koketkam,* to which Zagoskin's is a sequel), because she has heard it discussed by other characters and knows "there is a chambermaid in it very like me, though people complain she is too witty for a maid" (I, 5). Daša advises the hired playwright Erastov, who is writing the "comedy against comedy", that "there is nothing more difficult than to write a part for a maid. One person will say she is too stupid, another that she is too witty, and yet a third that she is always interrupting out of turn." If Erastov wishes to please his audience, Daša adds: "Your maid will not utter a word" (II, 3). The idea of a maid not uttering a word must have diverted Zagoskin's audience, though he – despite Daša's advice – never attempted this difficult technical feat. His chambermaids continue to play important parts in the intrigue, to advise, to comment and to deceive, just as all the other servant-girls had been doing on the stage since the 1760s.

That the audiences were equally well aware of the convention is demonstrated by the remarks of a contemporary critic on *Gore ot uma*. He praised Griboedov's comedy because "it contains no jesting servant, around whom the entire intrigue revolves".[31] Yet Griboedov followed tradition sufficiently to introduce into his play the witty and pert lady's maid Liza, capable of delivering epigrams and advising her mistress how to conduct a love affair. Liza's close relation to the soubrette of French comedy – rather than to the genuine servant-girl of Russian reality – is suggested by the failure of the celebrated producer Nemirovič-Dančenko to present her as a "simple serf girl" when he staged

[30] Felix Gaiffe, *op. cit.*, p. 388.
[31] A. M. Gordin, *op. cit.*, p. 19.

the play in 1910.[32] Liza is not as bold or as impertinent as some of her predecessors, even though Sofia has occasion to warn her not to allow herself too much freedom. Liza's declaration that she "cannot help loving the valet Petruška" is perhaps a derisive reference to the valet-chambermaid intrigue which runs parallel to the main intrigue in most comedies of the eighteenth century.

# VII

## Other Characters

For well over half a century, Russian playwrights manipulated the handful of stereotyped figures who populated the stage. Their ability to please audiences for so long with such limited means is a yard-stick of their ingenuity. No doubt the more talented of the writers were well aware of the limitations imposed upon them by these conventional puppets. But, after all, the gallery of types proved perfectly adequate for the moralising purpose of their plays, and as theatrical taste among the audiences became increasingly sophisticated, the playwrights began introducing other types taken from Russian reality. Some of these characters – merchants, itinerant hawkers, rustic match-makers – may derive partly from the "folk drama", farces or "intermediae".[33] Others represent characters familiar in more genteel society – poets, journalists, domestic tutors, foreigners. Clergy never appear, no doubt as a result of the censorship and the requirements of good taste, though Kutejkin appears with a "church book" in *Nedorosl'*, and Karpovič is said to have "failed in rhetoric at a seminary" (*Fom.*)[34]

Personages such as the workmen introduced in Lukin's *Ščepetil'nik* were unknown to Sumarokov and to French comedy of the classical period. However, Diderot declared in the 1750s that "representative members of various professions and social ranks" might well be made the subject of plays.[35] This suggestion was to lead in France to the development of the "comédie larmoyante", with its essentially middle-class environment.[36] In Russia, the introduction of types familiar to

[32] Boris Klejber, "Zagadki *Gorja ot uma*", *Scando-Slavica*, VII (1961), p. 31.
[33] B. N. Aseev, *op. cit.*, p. 126.
[34] In the 1830s P. A. Vjazemskij said of Fonvizin's Kutejkin: "No comic writer now would dare depict such a character to be laughed at by the audience", *op. cit.*, p. 30.
[35] Felix Gaiffe, *op. cit.*, p. 155.
[36] Discussed in Chapter III.

the audience from everyday life was more closely connected with Lukin's campaign for a more Russian and national content in stage plays, and with the opening of the galleries in public theatres.

The Russian merchant, as a figure of fun, first appears on the stage in the early 1780s. Černjavskij's *Kupečeskaja kompanija* ("Mercantile Company"), was rapidly followed by Kolčev's *Dvorjanjuščejsja kupets* ("Merchant into Gentleman", 1780) and its sequel, the anonymous *Peremena v nravax* ("A Change in Manners", 1789). In these plays, the merchant is a newly-rich tradesman anxious to buy his way into fashionable society, who is tricked and cheated by penniless aristocrats but who sees the folly of his behaviour in time for a happy denouement. The newly-rich snob reappears in Zagoskin's *Bogatonov,* where he undergoes similar experiences at the hand of the impoverished but fashionable Baroness Vol'mar. The merchant also appeared in comic operas, including Matinskij's *Sanktpeterburskij gostinnyj dvor* (1791).

Peasant were introduced more frequently into comic operas than into plays. They are depicted either as comic figures, or to illustrate the thesis that peasants were also capable of "sensibility". Faddei, the miller-magician of Ablesimov's Mel'nik-koldun diverts the audience with his quick wits and ingenuity, while the peasant hero and heroine of Plavil'ščikov's *Bobyl'* are depicted as sentimental lovers.

Early in the nineteenth century, audiences and critics began expressing their disapproval of the many comedies depicting "peasantry, soldiery and petty officials – who can only please the rabble".[37] The critics observed that the purpose of comedy was to "mock stupidity and the prejudices occurring in high society", and that this "high society" obtained no profit from knowing "what happens in taverns, country fairs and farms".[38] A critic writing in Karamzin's journal *Vestnik Evropy* in 1802 declared: "The rule of a writer of comedy is to entertain and provide benefit – yet what satisfaction is to be acquired by a well-born young lady from hearing a farmer quarrel with his wife, or one fool brawling with another, whose every word is intolerable to a refined ear?"[39] This complaint was echoed in 1805 by a writer in the *Žurnal russkoj slovesnosti* who inquired: "What pleasure can well-born ladies obtain from listening for a whole hour to the chatter of

[37] I. A. Krjažimskaja, "Iz istorii teatral'noj kritiki konca XVIII. – načala XIX. veka", in Akademija nauk S.S.S.R., *XVIII vek,* IV (1959), pp. 215-6.
[38] *Ibid.,* pp. 217-8.
[39] Akademija nauk S.S.S.R., *Istorija russkoj literatury,* V (Leningrad, 1941), p. 148.

village women?" – a criticism aimed against Plavil'ščikov's *Bobyl'*.[40]
This writer then suggested that two theatres should be established, one
for "gentry", the other for the "folk", each theatre to specialise in plays
appropriate to the taste of their audiences.

As a result of these and similar complaints, playwrights now began
introducing members of the aristocracy into their comedies with in-
creasing frequency. Earlier comedies had depicted an occasional count,
sometimes virtuous (as in *Obraščennyj mizantrop*), but more often an
unsuccessful suitor afflicted with a vice or foible; these included the
penniless counts of *Čudaki* and *Xvastun,* and the foolish countess
Trojkina of *Prokazniki,* who despises her step-brother because her own
father was gentry, and his was not (II, 3). In general, however, playwrights followed the example of Catherine, whose protagonists are
never higher in rank than mere gentry: significantly, the "bojar" of her
*Perednjaja znatnogo bojarina* ("The Eminent Boyar's Ante-chamber",
1772) does not appear in the play himself. Catherine is said to have
caricatured the Princess Daškova in a comedy, but it was not performed.[41] Apart from the impropriety of holding up members of the
aristocracy to public ridicule, the playwrights' avoidance of presenting
nobility in comedy was due to the care with which the classical rules
were observed: these did not admit elevated personages into the low
genre of comedy.

After 1815 the rules relaxed somewhat, and members of the aristocracy begin appearing in comedies. All the principal personages in
Šaxovskoj's comedies are titled, as they are in the plays of Zagoskin.
The only low persons are servants or episodic figures such as foolish
poets, blue-stockings or hack writers. Neither Čackij nor Famusov
have titles, but Famusov is an official in a government department,
and the guests at his evening party include a prince, his lady, and two
countesses.

Among the types who appear in the background of comedies included domestic tutors, usually introduced to illustrate the author's
views on faulty education. Foreigners, either ludicruous or immoral –
sometimes both – provided material for satirical attacks on Gallomania.
Bad poets and hack writers were often used as vehicles to attack rivals
or to parody a rival literary movement. These figures were always
subsidiary, though they are often portrayed with verve, skill and ingenuity.

[40]  Quoted by I. A. Krjažimskaja, *op. cit.,* p. 220.
[41]  V. V. Kallaš and N. E. Efros, *op. cit.,* p. 326.

## VIII

### *Methods of Characterising*

Restricted by their desire to moralise and divert, the writers of comedy were generally satisfied with conventional methods of characterising their personages. The portrayal of character through action was a device developed only later and by more sophisticated playwrights, whose concern was with the presentation of character rather than moralising. In the eighteenth century, the method most frequently employed was description, complemented by such devices as speaking names and the use of various kinds of vocabulary and phraseology.

Many characters in Russian comedy describe themselves, often in monologues. Sumarokov employed the monologue to reveal aspects of his miser Čužexvat's character which could not plausibly be depicted in dialogue or action. In *Opekun*, Čužexvat is accused by his ward of seeking to gain control of her fortune by marrying her against her will. Left alone, Čužexvat calls upon the Deity to witness that he "fears not the knout, but eternal torment", but follows this statement with the admission that he is trying to deceive God by "false logic" and in reality he has "not the least love either for Thee or for my neighbour". Lukin's toy-shop vendor soliloquises on his own charitable character: "I do not charge poor people high prices, for they earn their money by work; but I take it from the rich who – even without me – would still find a way to squander it" (sc. 5). This monologue is intended to establish the toy-shop vendor's character as a worthy citizen, and induce the audience to pay serious attention to his moralising.

Heroes and heroines reveal their feelings about one another in monologues. Sometimes these are "false monologues", in that a confidante is present; although the monologue is ostensibly addressed to the confidante, it is intended to inform the audiences of matters which could not be so easily conveyed in other ways. In any case, the purpose of these monologues is the same. Thus Sofia displays her own serious mind in a monologue as she reads and comments on Fénelon's "Education of Young Ladies" (*Ned.*, IV, 1). Ostromyslov describes his feelings and character in an extended monologue (*Fom.*, IV, 1). Servants also use monologues to inform the audience of their own ingenuity and sense: Mitrofan illustrates his peasant wit with a number of diverting Russian proverbs (*Fom.*, I, 1), so does Polist (*Xvastun*). Villains use monologues to expatiate on their own vices: Krivosudov admits his corruption in a monologue, during which he demands: "Am I then to watch pheasants fly past without seizing one for myself? I'd be a fool if I did!" (*Jab.*, I, 7). Xamkin declares his greed in a monologue: "Is there anything more beautiful than money? . . ." (Sokolov's *Sudeskie imeniny*). Rifmokrad boasts of the plagiarisms his speaking name suggests: "With the help of Racine and others, I write no worse than anyone else . . ." (*Prok.*, III, 5).

Monologues rarely extend to over ten lines, but the device was so useful for rendering personal feelings or thoughts to the audience, that it soon developed into the tirade. Eighteenth-century tragedy made copious use of the tirade, and an early instance occurs in Sumarokov's *Pustynnik* (1757), where irregular couplets help express the ebb and flow of feeling. Sumarokov's "short iambics" lead directly to Knjažnin, who used them in his comic-opera *Skupoj* (c. 1782). However, the tirade proper does not appear in comedy until playwrights took to writing them consistently in verse. Šaxovskoj made effective use of the verse tirade in *Urok koketkam*: the coquette Leleva delivers a long and witty set-piece of 34 lines – three times the length of the average prose monologue. During it, she exhibits to the audience aspects of her own character, as she dwells on her dislike for St.-Petersburg and delight in the society of Lipec Spa. Although Leleva's tirade is delivered in the presence of other characters, she does not address them. Like an operatic aria, it is intended for the audience, and Leleva holds up the play's action to give voice to her feelings after the fashion of an operatic heroine.

The link between tirades and verse comedy is demonstrated by the absence of tirades from Zagoskin's prose comedies, and their frequency in *Gora ot uma*. Here Griboedov surpasses his contemporaries yet again by the technical skill and theatrical effect of the device. Čackij expounds his attitude to Moscow society in 28 lines (I, 7), his "dangerous views" in 50 lines (II, 5), and again in 64 lines (III, 21). Famusov voices his opinions in 32 lines (II, 1 : III, 2). Repetilov reveals aspects of his character in 50 lines (IV, 4). These tirades are the equivalent of "false monologues" in prose comedy, mainly because the other characters present do not interrupt or even respond to them. On occasion, one of the other people present during the tirade will utter an aside (which the main speaker is not supposed to hear): Čackij's tirade against Moscow society is delivered while the other characters are "dancing or playing cards", and Čackij does not stop to consider whether anyone is listening. It is a measure of the originality of *Gore ot uma* that Griboedov was able to take this conventional device, which in the hands of less skilled playwrights does little more than hold up the action, and transform it by wit and poetry, while at the same time extracting the utmost effectiveness for characterisation.

The aside also enabled characters to express aspects of their personalities for the benefit of the audience. However, the aside was regarded (like the monologue) as artifical by French theoreticians, and this view was shared by Russian playwrights. Their uneasiness when employing asides during dialogue is apparent in the frequency with which a character in whose presence an aside has just been made will ask the character delivering the aside what he (or she) has just said (*Ščh.*, sc. 6, *Brig.*, I, 1, *Sbit.*, I, 6, and elsewhere).

Dialogue had long been recognised by verse satirists, starting with Horace, as a dramatic way of illustrating character. Verse satirists frequently made use of a dialogue between interlocutor and narrator, the former exposing the latter's vice or folly by means of a series of leading questions, exclamations of surprise, wonder or incredulity, all intended to provoke the narrator into betraying still more examples of his vice. This method was adopted by writers of comedy as a means for exposing their victims. Lukin's toy-shop vendor asks leading questions of the "petits-maîtres", giddy-pates and pedants who visit his shop, and this play clearly illustrates the relationship between "raisonneur" in comedy and the interlocutor of verse satire deliberately exposing his victim. Other characters who deliberately elicit instances of folly and vice from the playwright's target include the valet Polist (*Xvastun*), who is well aware of his master's boastful nature and even urges him: "take off your mask in front of one who knows how to distinguish any colour" (I, 7). Polist's role throughout this play is reminiscent of the interlocutor of verse satire, as he holds up his master Verxolet to the ridicule of the audience. Similarly, Mrs. Čvankina's maid elicits evidence of her mistress' follies and comments in asides upon it (II, 1).

Fonvizin used dialogue to great effect in *Brigadir*. However, instead of using the interlocutor-narrator device adapted from verse satire, he employed dialogues between two "negative" characters, each with a vice which the dialogue exposes. The comic effect obtained from these dialogues is intensified by ludicruous failures to understand. The Brigadir cannot understand his son who uses Franco-Russian salon jargon; the Brigadirša fails to understand the stilted official language used by the Sovetnik in his attempts to pay court to her. The Sovetnica derides the Brigadir's vocabulary and style when he seeks to flatter her. In *Nedorosl'*, the failure to respond or understand goes further: the virtuous characters rarely take the trouble to enter into dialogue with the Prostakov group.

Klušin's *Alximist* is a verse-satire dramatised and in form it resembles Juvenalian and Horatian satire introduced into Russia by Kantemir. Klušin's one-act comedy consists entirely of monologues by the alchemist Vskipjatalin, who corresponds to the interlocutor of verse satire (Horace, *Sermones*, I, 9 *The Bore* is the classical example). His function is to elicit information from a series of foolish characters who are the object of Klušin's satire. Rubakin, for instance, informs Vskipjatalin: "I am captain of cavalry Rubakin, aged 45, in the service since May 1st, 1751, wife and children have I none . . ." (sc. 2).

An extension of this somewhat primitive device for depicting character is the dialogue between two persons who are discussing or describing a third. Such exchanges often precede the entrance of the character under discussion. Knjažnin prepares the way for the entry of his diffident hero Prjat (*Čud.*), by a scene in which the heroine complains to her maid of his absurdly bashful nature: "For two years he has been in love with me, but never gave a sign . . . Not venturing to call upon us, though we have mutual friends, he always tries to waylay me when I am out walking, then will raise his hat and rush away . . ." (II, 1). Krylov uses the device to prepare for the appearance of Count Dubovid, the poet-taster of *Sočinitel' v prixozhei*: the Count's valet Andrej and the hack writer Rifmokrad discuss the Count's plagiarisms and liking for flattery, thus letting the audience know in advance what to expect when the Count himself appears. Kapnist opened *Jabeda* with a lengthy expository dialogue which serves to set the scene of the play and also to allow the Court secretary Dobrov to describe in some detail the characters of the various Court officials who are presently to make their appearances.

This method was still being used twenty years later. The first act of *Urok koketkam* consists entirely of a series of dialogues in which characters describe and discuss other characters before they appear. Saša the maid describes the coquette Leleva to the attendant Semeon; then she describes Ugarov and Fialkin to Xolmskij, and Xolmskij spends the next scene describing Ol'gin, the fashionable "umnik", for the benefit of Pronskij. Puškin criticised the "tedium" of these opening scenes,[42] but the device was too useful to abandon and occurs again in

---

[42] *Puškin v teatre* (Moscow, 1953), p. 304.

a number of plays. These include *Svoja sem'ja,* in which Mrs. Vel'du-zeva discourses wittily but lengthily on the characters of Felka and Nataša, after which she and Ljubim go on to discuss the rest of the characters (I, 2-4). Xmel'nitskij's *Šalosti vljublennyx* opens with a dialogue between heroine and her maid, describing the former's uncle and guardian, who is "strict, terribly jealous, cross and envious" (I, 1). When the uncle appears in the next scene he displays all these characteristics. Similarly, the heroine Prelesta and her maid discuss the "chatterbox" Zvonov, and decide he is a "great bore" (*Govorun,* "The Chatterbox", 1818). Xmel'nickij uses the device for comic effect, as Prelesta takes to her heels when the voice of Zvonov is heard at the end of the dialogue, immediately before he appears on the stage.

To present two characters describing a third in dialogue is perhaps one of the simplest methods of characterisation in dramaturgy. It was left to Griboedov, however, to make such dialogues serve other purposes as well. *Gore at uma* was praised by the contemporary critic O. M. Somov because (among other things) the first scene "does not introduce a valet and maid, or two other persons, to explain to the audience the characters of the main personages".[43] Griboedov postpones the inevitable scene in which the hero is discussed by the heroine and her maid until the fifth scene of Act I, by which time the audience have been shown that Sofia is already in love with the unsuitable Molčalin. Čackij is thus identified as Molčalin's rival as well as the play's hero. A less skilful playwright would have opened his comedy with this scene.

Characterisation through action which revealed or illuminated some aspect of a personage was rarely attempted by eighteenth-century playwrights. Action on the stage was regarded primarily as a means of providing laughter by comic effects of the kind found in farce – brawls, misunderstandings, quarrels, disguises and the like. Only Fonvizin succeeded in using action to depict character; the opening scenes of *Nedorosl'* depict Mitrofan being measured for a coat, and this incident, trivial though it is, enables Fonvizin to show (instead of merely describing) Mrs. Prostakova's callous attitude to the servants, her fondness for the ignorant "minor" her son, her coarse behaviour towards her own husband and brother. All these characters are brought in and contribute something to the incident, which is shown and not merely narrated. Similarly, Mrs. Prostakova's reactions to Sofia, when the latter hears she is an heiress, illuminate her character; and when

43 A. M. Gordin, ed., *op. cit.,* p. 19.

Starodum appears Prostakova gazes at him "with slavish humility" (III, 5) despite his reluctance to submit to her embrace. But Fonvizin's contemporaries and successors did not feel the need to make action an organic part of character-portrayal, because their interests lay elsewhere. Not until *Gore ot uma* did Griboedov succeeded in revealing through incident and action those aspects of his characters which could not be revealed so economically or effectively by plain description. The most striking instance of Griboedov's skill in this respect, especially when compared with his predecessors, occurs in the play's denouement: here the climax to the intrigue involving Sofia, Čackij and Molčalin is presented in a "tragic collision" [44] during which Čackij, concealed from the other characters behind a pillar though his presence is known to the audience, watches as Sofia discovers Molčalin's falsity. The dramatic tension generated by this situation mounts until Čackij's reveals himself, Liza "drops the candle in alarm", Molčalin "takes refuge in his room" and Sofia bursts into tears (IV, 13). The disturbance caused by this incident brings Famusov and "a crowd of servants with candles" to the scene, leading to Čackij's final tirade and departure. This series of scenes which combine incident, action, character-portrayal and plot far surpass in theatrical interest the work of Griboedov's contemporaries – the more so as the force of the denouement derives from social differences as much as from "psychological incompatibility" and conflict.[45]

# IX

## Language

A more immediately effective method of portraying characters was that of endowing them with speech peculiarities which the audience could recognise as typical of a class or calling. Characters could be made to use the phraseology and vocabulary of the "petits-maîtres" and giddy-pates, or of merchants, peasants, provincial gentry, officials or military men. The use of vernacular, inadmissable in elevated genres, was well suited to comedy as Molière had demonstrated by his peasants in *Don Juan* or *M. de Pourceaugnac*, speaking their native

[44]   Bertha Malnick, "The theory and practice of Russian drama in the early 19th century", *Slavonic and East European Review*, 34 (1955), p. 14.
[45]   *Ibid.*, p. 14.

*patois*, or by his physicians with their pseudo-Latin jargon. In any case, Lukin's campaign for increased national awareness in the Russian theatre favoured the use of colloquial, natural Russian speech, of folk words and sayings which reflected Russian reality. But in the 1790s the use of such speech in comedy was increasingly attacked by critics, who protested at the coarseness of the Russian stage in contrast to the elegance of the French. The refined "blagorodnaja komedija" of the 1810s came into being partly in reaction to the earlier vulgarity of certain playwrights.

Characters in Russian comedy can usually be recognised for what they are by the language they speak. Heroes, heroines and "raisonneurs" use an elevated, often stilted terminology. They make frequent references to "heart", "feeling", "sense", "virtue" and "sensibility". Čistoserdov in Lukin's *Ščepetil'nik* provides early examples of the elaborate syntax and diction characteristic of these people. He is fond of aphorisms: "Weaknesses and passions occur in people of all conditions of life, though the eyes of the populace always turn to an eminent person, and faults in such are always more apparent than in those of less eminence" (sc. 1). The scenes between Sofia and Dobroljubov (*Brig.*) are couched in refined and stilted language which provides a contrast to the colloquial, even coarse language of the Brigadir and the affected Franco-Russian jargon of Ivan and the Sovetnica. Fonvizin's skilful use of various kinds of utterance and vocabulary in *Brigadir* was developed still further in *Nedorosl'*, where each of the main personages is clearly differentiated from the others by his or her manner of speech. Starodum's old-fashioned bookish style and vocabulary contrasts with the refined speech of Pravdin; Mrs. Prostakova uses different styles of speech when she addresses Starodum and when she speaks to the servants; the three domestic tutors are differentiated by the language they employ – Kutejkin's clerical background is suggested by his use of Old Church Slavonic terms, while Cyfirkin uses military phraseology as an old soldier, and the foreigner Vral'man has a pronounced German accent.

"Official" language, sometimes parodied, was quickly recognised by audiences. Fonvizin's Sovetnik uses chancellery terms, Krjučkodej addresses his bride as though she were a law-court (*SPD*, II, 4-5), and Kapnist introduced a parody of a Court document, couched in the appropriate style, into *Jabeda* (V, 2).

The most used specific phraseology in Russian comedy was the Franco-Russian jargon first introduced by Sumarokov in *Ssora* (1750).

But in reality, the salon jargon was more varied than the examples provided by Sumarokov or even Lukin.[46] The jargon consisted not only of a French word or phrase inserted into a Russian sentence, but also of the addition of Russian grammatical endings to French words, Russian words accentuated as though French, calques and literal translations from French into Russian of entire phrases. Thus such words and phrases occur: "on amuritsja", "dlja amuru", "kurjozna" (*Ned.*, II, 4, 6), "delikates moego sluxa" (*Nesčastie*, II, 5), "dimavez jumer" (i.e. de mauvais humeur) (*Obr. miz.*, III, 3), "vy flatiruete" (*Čud.*, II, 3), "que mysli vous avez so mnoju odinaki" (*ib.*, II, 3), "veritables priznaki" (*ib.*) and "pikiruetes" (*ib.*). Mistakes in Russian were used for comic effect and emphasize the stupidity of a character: "xvamilija" (*RiL*, III, 3), "pereminaž" (i.e. "promenade" confused with "pereminat'sja") (*SPD*, II, 5) and "nekruty" (*Bob.*, I, 8).

The introduction of peasantry into comedies or comic operas gave the playwrights scope for ingenuity in their use of language to stress the social origin of these characters. The terminology used by peasants on the stage ranges from conventional greetings such as "zdorovo, krasotka, zdrovo!" (*RiL*, I, 2), endearments ("duša moja!", "ljubeznaja moja nevesta!"), exclamations ("fu!", "ču!", "ux!") to diminuitives ("prostuška moja!") and oaths or imprecations. These were particularly frequent, and include "tfu propast!", "tfu k čortu!", "Satana tebja poberi, prokljatyj!", and "ty kanal'ja boronovolok!". Insults included "povesa!", "staraja negodjajka!", "sundurščica" and "bezdelnik". Prostakova's coarse nature is shown by her use of such low words as "skot!", "bestija", "staraja ved'ma", and "sobač'ja ty doč!"

Some playwrights gave their peasant characters speeches which included phonetic, morphological and lexical examples of genuine peasant usage. Lukin's two workmen in *Sčepetil'nik* employ "tsokanie", "dzekanie", "akanie" and "i" in place of "jat". Other dialect words used for comic effect and "placing" peasant characters include: "robjata" (*RiL*, I, 7), "lix ja ne vernyj", "lix on moj ženix", "oščo" and "eščo" (*ib.*, II, 3-4). The peasant who appears in Fonvizin's *Korion* uses the enclitic "-sta", frequently employed later by other writers who "thought it sounded like peasant speech".[47]

Peasant in comedy often give voice to Russian sayings and folk aphorisms: "vit on ne volk, ne ukusit" (*RiL*, II, 4), "vit do Boga

[46] K. V. Pigarev, *Tvorčestvo Fonvizina* (Moscow, 1954), p. 106.
[47] P. N. Berkov, *Russkaja komedija i komičeskaja opera* (Moscow-Leningrad, 1950), p. 19.

vysoko, a do carja daleko" (*ib.*, III, 5), "ne pljun v poganoj kolodec, slučitsja vodicy ispit'" (*ib.*, III, 6), "kak stariki moj mcnja ne uvidjat, to pojdet dym koromyslom" (*Mel.*, II, 1), "dela ne delaj, ot dela ne begaj" (*Ned.*, III, 6), "ja v svoem rode ne poslednij" (*ib.*, IV, 7), "gol, kak ladon" (*Jabeda*, I, 1), "staryj drug ... lučše novyx dvux" (*ib.*), "čto vzjato, to svjato" (*Fom.*, I, 1). Such sayings as these were also put into the mouths of valets and chambermaids, implying that these characters were well endowed with native good sense and wit.

However, objections were made to the copious use of folk dialect and coarse phrases from the vernacular language. In 1777 Nikolev objected to the dialect forms used by G. R. Deržavin in *Duročka* (1776) and by L'vov in *Jamščiki* ("The Coachmen", 1777). To prevent such criticism being aimed at his own comic operas on peasant themes, Nikolev set *Rozana i Ljubim* "near Moscow", to avoid the "savage speech" of "steppe peasantry", which might offend the refined taste of his audience.[48] Consequently Nikolev's peasantry use a stylised "stage rustic" later employed by other writers of comic opera including Krylov, whose peasants in *Kofejnica* speak a stylised peasant language. Although Plavil'ščikov also used "stage rustic" for his peasantry in *Bobyl'*, the play was attacked by critics for its "deliberate use of coarse expressions".[49] Similarly, Šaxovskoj and Zagoskin were attacked in the 1810s for "vulgar expressions" and "expressions suited only to a cavalry regiment", while at the same time other critics condemned them for using too many Gallicisms.[50] The natural, witty and elegant language used by Griboedov in *Gore ot uma* was yet another of the features which made the play stand out against the background of contemporary dramaturgy; but that aspect of the play goes beyond the scope of this essay.

---

[48] Quoted in P. N. Berkov, *Russkaja komedija i komičeskaja opera XVIII v.*, p. 172.
[49] I. A. Krjažimskaja, *op. cit.*, Akademija nauk S.S.S.R., *XVIII v.*, IV (1959), p. 218.
[50] Akademija nauk S.S.S.R., *Istorija russkoj literatury*, V (Leningrad, 1941), p. 304; N. I. Mordovčenko, *Russkaja kritika pervoj četverti XIX v.* (Moscow, 1959), pp. 238-9.

## III.  GENRE AND STRUCTURE

### The "Comédie de caractère"

The "great, grand and prestige-laden" genres of the eighteenth century were the epic, tragedy and ode, supported by an "immense body of critical theory, each with appropriate subjects and a style suited to it".[1] Comedy, which eventually came to embrace nearly all the forms of non-tragic dramaturgy, was below these genres in the hierarchy and was therefore more open to contamination by other strains, from the sentimental to the operatic. The French theatre recognised a wide range of kinds of comedy, most of which found their way to the Russian stage. These kinds included the "comédie de caractère", the "comédie de moeurs", the "comédie larmoyante", and less well-defined species such as the "comédie personelle", the "comédie historique", the "comédie politique" and others.[2]

Of these kinds, the "comédie de caractère" as perfected by Molière was the most highly regarded, and retained its prestige in France until the end of the eighteenth century, although by this time it had in practice fallen into desuetude. The aim of a writer of a "comédie de caractère" was to incarnate a complete human type, a universal character; this type provided the play with its focus and at the same time the type personified a human vice, fault or foible. Eighteenth-century theoreticians declared that this central character should "produce an inevitable crisis in the action" of the play, and this action should itself be devised in such a way as to illustrate the vice, fault or foible satirised.

The plot therefore was to "consist of a series of appropriate retributions for the variations from a norm which was represented" by the

---

[1] Hugh Maclean, "The development of modern Russian literature", *Slavic Review*, 21 (1962), p. 392.
[2] F. V. Fournel, *Le théâtre au XVII siècle: la comédie* (Paris, 1892), p. 152.

character.[3] In addition, the true "comédie de caractère" was expected to bear a title indicating who this central character was, and the vice to be satirised in the play. Molière's *l'Avare, le Misanthrope* and *le Malade imaginaire* provided eighteenth-century writers in both Western Europe and in Russia with models of the "comédie de caractère", since these plays exhibited all the required features.

Molière's authority remained high in Russia throughout the eighteenth century. The claim that "Molière found his second homeland in Russia"[4] is supported by the number of translations and adaptations which appeared there. More than twenty of his plays were produced in the 1760s, either in Russian adaptations or in French. Novikov's printing-house alone published thirteen translations from Molière, some going into second editions, in as many years.[5] Plays by Molière's successors and imitators such as Regnard, Destouches and Gresset were almost as popular, and continued to be produced in Russia (as in France) as late as 70 years after the first productions in Paris. Lukin adapted plays by Regnard between 1763 and 1765, though Regnard died in 1710 and his most popular plays date from the 1690s. Elagin translated most of the comedies of Destouches in the 1780s (originally performed between 1710 and 1732). However, many of the "comédies de caractère" by these French writers continued to hold the stage in Paris until the Revolution of 1789 – a fact which suggests the prestige they still held for audiences.

Nevertheless, Molière had almost exhausted the limited range of the "comédie de caractère", and his successors saw this. Once the seven deadly sins and most of the lesser human vices and foibles had been personified and satirised on the stage, the playwrights realised their subjects had run out. It was in any case impossible to improve on Molière's handling of these subjects. The same process occurred in Restoration England at this time, where the English equivalent of the "comédie de caractère" – the Elizabethan and post-Elizabethan comedy of humours – also became pale and exhausted by the 1690s.

As the titles of Destouches' "comédies de caractère" indicate, he was reduced by the early 1700s to satirising superficial foibles and oddities of behaviour; these plays include *Le Curieux impertinent*

[3]  Dudley H. Miles, *The influence of Molière on Restoration comedy* (New York, 1910), p. 32.
[4]  Jules Patouillet, "Molière et sa fortune en Russie", *Revue des études slaves*, 2 (1922), p. 272.
[5]  V. F. Semennikov, *Knigoizdatel'skaja dejatel'nost' N. I. Novikova* (Petersburg, 1921). This lists Novikov's publications by year.

(1710), *L'Irrésolu* (1713) and *Le Glorieux* (1732). The French stage was crowded for over a century with comedies satirising mere foibles and eccentricities; they ranged from *Le Grondeur* (Brueys, 1691), *Le Flatteur* (J.-B. Rousseau, 1696), *Le Distrait* (Regnard, 1697), *Le Capricieux* (J.-B. Rousseau, 1700), *Le Méchant* (Gresset, 1745) to *L'Indécis* (Charbonnière, 1812). Lessing protested in 1767 that "an absent-minded man deserves ridicule as little as one who has the headache",[6] but these "irrésolus, dissipateurs, indiscrets *et hoc genus omnes*" were "to revolve about themselves like squirrels in a cage" until the French Revolution, and after.[7] They continued to make their appearance on the Russian stage until the 1820s.

Molière's genius "paralysed two generations of French dramatists",[8] and comedy, as a means of literary expression, ceased attracting the best contemporary French playwrights. Unable to complete with their great predecessor, professional playwrights in France began between 1700 and 1730 to turn their attention instead to plot and situation. Diderot, who admitted "there are at most only a dozen truly comic 'characters' marked with 'grands traits' ",[9] made it clear in the 1750s that in his view the construction of plot should be the main concern of playwrights. His plays and theoretical writings were known and studied with interest in Russia in the 1760s by Elagin and the group of playwrights and translators who worked for him.

The technique propounded by Diderot was generally adopted by Russian writers of the "comédie de caractère", although Sumarokov, the leading exponent of classical genres based on French models, founded a number of his comedies directly upon plays by Molière; they included *Pridanoe obmanom* (le Malade imaginaire), *Pustaja ssora Vzdorščica* (les Précieuses ridicules, les Fâcheux), and *Rogonosec* (le Cocu imaginaire). Knjažnin, Sumarokov's follower, based his two most ambitious comedies *Xvastun* and *Čudaki* on du Brieux's *L'Important* (1723) and Destouches' *L'Homme singulier* (1764) respectively. In these plays, Sumarokov and Knjažnin place their central characters in a series of diverting situations which do not, however, evolve naturally from the central character's ruling passion.

Persistent interest in Molière in Russia is illustrated by the number of translations which continued to appear well into the early nineteenth

---

[6] Gotthold Efraim Lessing, *Hamburg dramaturgy*, no. 28 (1767).
[7] F. C. Green, *Minuet* (London, 1935), p. 152.
[8] *Ibid.*, p. 152.
[9] Denis Diderot, *Writings on the theatre*, ed. F. C. Green (Cambridge, 1936), p. 89.

century.[10] Almost all the more talented playwrights adapted one or more of Molière's comedies; Kapnist translated *Sgnarelle* in 1780 and revised it in 1806. More translations of all Molière's more important plays appeared in the 1810s.[11] Krylov's *Urok dočkam* (1806) owed its subject to Molière, and even the use of the word "urok" in the title derives from the fashion introduced by Molière for titles including the words *L'École*. . . . In 1814, despite political events, there was a production of *Les Fourberies de Scapin* in St.-Petersburg, and *Le Misanthrope* was "adapted to Russian manners" in 1816 by Kokoškin. Šaxovskoj acknowledged his debt to Molière in the creation of certain of his characters, though in his view Molière's finest comedies were not "comédies de caractère" at all, but comedies of manners.[12] Like Krylov, Šaxovskoj also used the word "urok" in titles such as *Urok koketkam* and *Urok ženatym* ("A Lesson to the Married", 1823). Zagoskin, too, owes a debt to Molière in his comedies dealing with gullible, newly-rich Bogatonov. His *Komedija protiv komedii ili Urok volokitam,* written in defence of and as commentary on *Urok koketkam* resembles Molière's *Critique de l'École des femmes* in this respect. His *Večernika učenyx* resembles *Les Femmes savantes* in theme. Even Xmel'nickij, celebrated for his "hautes comédies", shared the enthusiasm for Molière, and translated *Tartuffe* and *L'École des femmes,* while his *Nerešitel'nyj* ("The Undecided", 1820) derives in part from *L'Irrésolu,* by Destouches – one of Molière's leading imitators.

Griboedov's indebtedness to Molière and to the classical "comédie de caractère" is less immediately apparent than in the work of his contemporaries. But critics soon saw resemblances between Čackij and Alceste, both "tragic figures beset by trivialities".[13] Both were "unreasonable, tactless in their outbursts, egocentric, petulant", and both provide the central action of the respective comedies by "repeated attempts to discover the true feelings of the heroine" towards him.[14] Even the "moral" of *Gore ot uma* is as ambiguous as that of *Le Misanthrope*. One of the central themes in the "comédies de caractère" of Molière is also treated in *Gore ot uma* – imperviousness to truth.[15]

[10] Jules Patouillet, *op. cit.*, pp. 272-90.
[11] B. S. Mejlax, ed., *Russkie dramaturgi XVIII-XIX vv.*, II (Leningrad, 1961), p. 21.
[12] Preface to *Polubarskie zatei* (1820), quoted by N. I. Mordovčenko, *Russkaja kritika pervoj četverti XIX v.* (Moscow, 1959), p. 246.
[13] J. D. Hubert, *Molière and the comedy of intellect* (Stanford, 1962), p. 139.
[14] *Ibid.*, pp. 139, 144.
[15] Further analogies are quoted by Jules Patouillet, "Molière et sa fortune en Russie", *Revue des études slaves*, 2 (1922), pp. 288-9.

In Russia, however, the native "comédie de caractère" was never as popular with audiences as comedies of situation or manners, or the "comédie larmoyante". In 1765 Lukin declared: "Only a small part of the audience likes comedies of character, filled with affecting and noble thoughts – the other, main section prefers diverting comedies." [16] In any case, this "small part" of the audience was able to indulge its tastes at the French theatre in St.-Petersburg, inaccessible to the audiences of pit and gallery in the public theatres. But it was the didactic element inseparable from the "comédie de caractère" which made these plays less popular than the "diverting comedies". Certainly the moralising in Šaxovskoj's plays made fashionable society in the capital prefer the "hautes comédies" of Xmel'nickij and the like.

Thus, despite the prestige of Molière and the "comédie de caractère", no Russian playwright of this period succeeded in producing a "native" comedy of character; instead, the writers preferred applying their skill and talent to comedies of manners, in which characters need only possess the charm of actuality, and in which contemporary type-characters could be substituted for the "general" human types depicted in the comedy of character.

## II

### The Comedy of Manners

The Russian comedy of manners, known as "bytovaja komedija" or "komedija nravov", differed essentially from the comedy of manners practised in France by such writers as Dancourt or Marivaux, and by the playwrights of the English Restoration. The French writers "held the mirror up to the follies and foibles of society without assuming the frown of a judge or uttering the jeer of a satirist".[17] The English playwrights, on the other hand, were mainly concerned in their comedies with sexual *mœurs* and with changes in the social structure of their time.[18] The Russian "komedija nravov" was primarily satirical. The Russian playwrights were preoccupied with the depiction of contemporary manners, customs, ways and habits – with the purpose of cor-

---

[16]   L. Ja. Gurevič, *Istorija russkogo teatral'nogo byta*, I (Moscow, 1934), p. 101.
[17]   Dudley H. Miles, *op. cit.*, p. 33.
[18]   John C. Loftis, *Comedy and society: Congreve to Fielding* (Stanford, 1954) deals with this topic in detail.

recting what was faulty in them by mockery. In this respect, the "komedija nravov" has much in common with the "comédie de caractère" – with the essential difference, however, that the "komedija nravov" was aimed at contemporary society – or at certain classes of it – while the "comédie de caractère" took as its target a single human fault common to all men.

The first Russian comedies of manners were produced during the 1764-65 season in St.-Petersburg. One was Lukin's *Ščepetiľnik*, into which he introduced specifically Russian social customs, such as the St.-Petersburg public masquerade during which the action of the play takes place, the use of Russian money (sc. 9), a Russian dialect spoken by the two workmen and portraits of Russian types familiar in contemporary society of the capital. Fonvizin's *Korion,* also produced in this season, contains several elements of "local colour" later to become characteristic of the comedy of manners as the genre was understood in Russia. Fonvizin's play is a version of Gresset's "comédie larmoyante" *Sidney* (1745), which depicts a "young lover consumed with melancholy, haunted by the idea of suicide".[19] Fonvizin transformed this into a comedy of manners by the ingenious addition of "bytovoj" traits of Russian life; these included the use of Slavonic names, a Russian serf-valet called Andrej, references to "merry-making in Moscow", the sound of Moscow church-bells and satirical references to "preferment" in the government service.

The addition of such "bytovoj" details to adaptations and translations of French plays was one of the main tenets of Lukin and his followers in their campaign to adapt plays to Russian manners. Fonvizin ventured still further into the comedy of manners with "bytovoj" detail in his next play, *Brigadir*. The stage setting of this play is remarkably detailed:

A room furnished in a rural manner. The Brigadir in a long coat, smoking tobacco. His son in "déshabillé" sulking and drinking tea. The Sovetnik, in a Cossack coat, is looking at a calendar. .... A table with tea things, at which the Sovetnica is sitting, in "déshabillé", wearing a cornet and pouring tea in an affected manner. The Brigadir's wife is sewing a stocking, and Sofia embroidering a tambour.

This opening tableau, in which all the main characters of the play are caught "off guard" and at home, instead of the usual pair of servants, as well as the stage directions as to costume, setting and such detail as the Sovetnik's calendar (or almanach) were an innovation on the Rus-

---

[19]   Felix Gaiffe, *op. cit.*, p. 33.

sian stage. Hitherto, plays had been set in a "room" or even "a house". Sumarokov, for instance, gives no directions as to stage settings in his early plays, and even Lukin's *Ščepetil'nik*, for all its "bytovoj" detail, is set against the featureless background of "a large room with tables and chairs, candelabra on the walls". Its setting alone made *Brigadir* a startling novelty to the audiences of the 1760s and 1770s. Other details from contemporary reality include the natural language used by the characters, heard here for the first time on the Russian stage.[20] The characters adress one another by first name and patronymic (Akulina Timofejevna, Avdot'ja Potapevna, Ignatej Andreevič and the like), or by terms of endearment such as "matuška", "batjuška", "soseduška" or "bratec". Even the game of cards in act IV requires the players to use Russian terminology.

Skilful and original as they are, these are merely superficial details. More significant was the way in which Fonvizin succeeded for the first time in depicting on the stage aspects of Russian manners and customs. Essentially, the Brigadir and his wife epitomise provincial gentry whose way of life has itself been responsible for the ignorant and foolish nature of their son Ivan, and for the tyranny they exercise over their serfs. The Sovetnik and his wife, on the other hand, epitomise minor gentry from St.-Petersburg, although as the Sovetnica insists, they are "all gentry and all equal" (I, 1). The "positive" characters in the play also represent a specific group in Russian society. They are the "new people", concerned with education and enlightenment in their own country, unaffected by cosmopolitan foibles and follies, and hence contrasted with the backward provincials and minor gentry from the capital. That Fonvizin's characters were "recognised" by the audience as belonging to their own society is attested by Panin's remark: *"Brigadir* is the first comedy on our manners."[21] The effect of the play is illustrated by the way in which the rank of "brigadir" was thereafter demoted to a "laughable appelation", though the rank itself was no more comic than any other.[22]

Sumarokov was clearly influenced by the methods of Lukin and Fonvizin in his later plays (after 1765). Although his *Rogonosec* (1772) was adapted from Molière, it is set in a "provincial manor house", and the central characters Vikul and his wife Xavron'ja are pre-occupied with domestic matters, eating and drinking, and enter-

[20]  P. A. Vjazemskij, *op. cit.*, p. 134.
[21]  Quoted by K. V. Pigarev, *op. cit.*, p. 103.
[22]  P. A. Vjazemskij, *op. cit.*, p. 135.

taining visitors in a hospitable manner. The action of Sumarokov's *Tri brata sovmestniki,* also an adaptation from the French, has been transposed to Moscow, the characters have Russian names (Ol'ga, Svjatoslav), and there is a reference to the near-by "Andreevskii monastery". Russian proverbs replace the French sayings of the original. O'her "everyday" Russian elements which Sumarokov introduced into his later plays included references to Catherine's Commission for the new Code of Laws (in *Opekun*), to her decree prohibiting rates of interest on loans higher than six per cent (*Pridanoe obmanon* and *Lixoimec*), while the Battle of Bender is mentioned in *Mat' sovmestnica dočeri* ("The Mother her Daughter's Confidante"), and a character in *Vzdorščica* is depicted wearing a "konfederatka" cap, as worn by troops in the Bar Confederation of 1768-72.[23]

Catherine's early comedies were sub-titled "komedii nravov" by her ninetenth-century editor,[24] and another critic declared that her plays were "taken from a wide ocean of existence".[25] Catherine used the plays to satirise the critical gentry of Moscow, derides their views on contemporary education, manifestations of Gallomania and their abuse of authority over serfs. Mrs. Xanžaxina declares, for instance, that servants "have no right to dream of family life" (*O Vremja!*). References to everyday details also occur in these plays, such as a decree against high interest rates (*O Vremja!*, I, 1) and the "Monthly collection" – the first Russian journal. Russian money is used, as well as Russian sayings ("The apple falls not far from the apple-tree", *ib.*, I, 12). Novikov expressed great admiration for Catherine's *O Vremja!*, which he called "the first comedy written precisely on our manners".[26]

In her later plays (1786-91), Catherine abandoned the comedy of manners, perhaps from reluctance to compete with Fonvizin, and concentrated instead on satire attacking her opponents (Novikov, Cagliostro, Gamalei) in comedies displaying little interest in contemporary Russian customs and manners. Her attempt to transfer Shakespeare's *The Merry Wives of Windsor* to Russian manners was not a success.

"Bytovoj" details appear in the setting, costumes and manners depicted in Kolyčev's *Dvorjanjušisja kupec* (1780), which includes a card-game and a dancing lesson. Eighteen months later the Russian comedy

[23] P. Rulin, "Elementy zlobodnevnosti v komedijax A. P. Sumarokova", *Slavia*, 4 (1925-6), pp. 720-738.
[24] A. A. Vvedenskij.
[25] A. S. Arxangel'skij, "Dramaturgija ekaterinskoj epoxi", in *Istorija russkogo teatra*, I, ed. by V. V. Kallaš and N. E. Efros (Moscow, 1914), p. 264.
[26] A. Afanas'jev, *Russkie satiričeskie žurnaly* (Moscow, 1859), p. 98.

of manners attained the height of its development in the eighteenth-century theatre with the first production of Fonvizin's *Nedorosl'*. This play too has been called the "first comedy of manners" in the Russian theatre.[27] As Gogol' pointed out, the most significant aspect of this play – and of *Brigadir* – was their "genuinely social" content.[28] In addition to a wealth of "bytovoj" detail, *Nedorosl'* also depicts a number of typically Russian characters, of whom Prostakova, for one, exhibits "all the traits of her class, country and period".[29] The satirical element, characteristic of the Russian comedy of manners, is emphasised throughout the play and it is directed against Russian society, rather than against the general human failings attacked by Catherine. The play's "typically Russian" characters and characteristics help explain why it is the only eighteenth-century comedy still in the current repertory.

One of the many imitations of *Nedorosl'* was Kopev's *Obraščennyj mizantrop,* and this play follows Fonvizin's comedy in its use of a "bytovoj" setting; the stage directions to Act I require the representation of "Gur Filatič's rural chamber", with pictures "from the Spasskij bridge, such as Bova Korolevič and the Battle of Mamaev" on the walls. The fourth act takes place during the Lebedjanskij market and fair, and depicts the market actually in progress.

Knjažnin, as a follower of Sumarokov rather than Lukin and Fonvizin, made use of little "bytovoj" detail in his comedies, which are closest to comedy of situation. However, his *Xvastun* treats a theme from contemporary Russian life – the acquisition of title and rank by bribery or influence. *Čudaki* also satirises the Gallomania fashionable in Russian society, and the "philosophising" derived from the same source. It was in his comic operas that Knjažnin was able to deal more fully with such "bytovoj" characters as Russian peasants, provincial gentry, merchants and even a seller of "sbiten". These personages all use dialect forms of speech, or the Franco-Russian jargon, or a stilted "literary" language, according to their position in society. In addition, Knjažnin's plays and comic operas contain copious examples of Russian proverbs and sayings, as well as aphorisms of Kjnažnin's own invention which later became proverbial in their own right. However, Knjažnin foresaw the decline of the genuine comedy of manners, when

[27]   N. I. Mordovčenko, *op. cit.*, p. 248.
[28]   N. V. Gogol', "V čem že nakonec suščestvo russkoj poèzii ...", in his *Polnoe sobranie sočinenij*, VIII (Leningrad, 1952), p. 396.
[29]   V. I. Pokrovskij, ed., *Fonvizin – žizn' i sočinenija* (SPb., 1903), p. 155.

he wrote: "Earlier, comedy meant the comedy of manners – now comedy is nothing but a school of wit." [30]

The use of "bytovoj" detail in comedies and comic opera was partly responsible for the criticisms levelled against them of "coarseness" [31] and such criticism was no doubt one of the reasons why the comedy of manners underwent the decline already observed by Knjažnin. However, Šaxovskoj and Zagoskin revived the genre in the 1810s and later. They continued to use Russian settings for their plays, but tended to exclude low persons such as peasants or rustics, or to use them merely as secondary figures. The "bytovoj" details introduced into their comedies were those of polite society: games of boston, whist, grand-patience, a troupe of gipsies to entertain guests, a dinner-party on the stage (*Bogatonov v stolice*, act II), references to such popular reading as Lévêque's *Histoire de la Russie*, the fashion for literary soirées, theatre-going and parties with fireworks (*Urok koketkam*).

Several characteristics of the Russian comedy of manners appear in *Gore ot uma*, with its satire against "depraved and pharisaical" Moscow society, its typically Russian characters from that society who attend Famusov's evening party, and the Moscow setting with all its references. Pushkin saw this aspect of the play very clearly when he described it as a "sharp picture of manners".[32] But the play is much more than a traditional comedy of manners on the Russian model, with the familiar characters and setting recognisable in the plays of Šaxovskoj. Its social significance, which relates *Gore ot uma* to the plays of Fonvizin, must have been as startling to readers and audiences of the time as *Nedorosl'* forty years earlier. This social significance in *Gore ot uma* was skilfully emphasised by Griboedov's use of the colloquial vocabulary and phraseology of fashionable Moscow society, references to the secret societies which flourished in the 1810s and to the practise of "informing". The representation on the stage of an evening party with music and dancing, and the use of these scenes as a background to the action of the play were also highly original. The political implications of the play have been examined in detail by Ključevskij and later writers,[33] and analogies have been seen with the first Polish "political comedy" – J. U. Niemcewicz' *Powrót posła* ("The Return of the

---

[30] B. N. Vsevolodskij-Gerngross, *Russkij teatr vtoroj poloviny XVIII v.* (Moscow, 1960), p. 280.

[31] See above, p. 87.

[32] Letter to A. A. Bestužev, January 1825.

[33] Vl. Orlov, "Xudožestvennaja problematika Griboedova", *Lit. nasledstvo*, 47-8 (Moscow, 1946), p. 20.

Deputy", 1791) – which Griboedov may have seen while in Poland.[34] However this may be, contemporary audiences certainly caught the political implications in the conflict between Čackij and Famusov, representatives of the "new" and "old" generations, which the censorship overlooked.

*Gore ot uma* also transcends the traditional eighteenth-century comedy of manners in that critical interest in the play during the last hundred years has transferred from its "bytovoj" scenes to Čackij's "spiritual drama" [35] an aspect unknown to the heroes of earlier comedy. In any case, the play does not conform to the genre in content or structure. Puškin, among others, declared that the play was "mixed" [36] in content: it is a romantic comedy, displaying various elements from satire to a realistic picture of contemporary manners. It represented a break with the classical respect for genre and rules, and in this respect too is a precursor of the "romantic" in dramaturgy.


# III


## *The Comedy of Situation*


The comedy of situation in the Russian theatre was usually founded on a simple intrigue provided by the efforts of servants to place obstacles in the way of foolish or disagreeable suitors, and to encourage the courtship of their master or mistress. Sumarokov's early *Ssora u muža* had provided a formula for the comedy of situation, from which few of his successors departed very far. The intrigue of this one-act comedy (which borders on farce) depicts an ingenious valet deceiving two foolish suitors, each of whom is supported by a husband and wife respectively. Taking this situation as a basis, later playwrights proceeded to introduce variations into it. Sometimes the valet's place is taken by a maid-servant. The valet or maid may further the deception by disguising him or herself, as in Sumarokov's *Vzdorščica*, where the valet Rozmarin in disguise frightens Mrs. Burda into allowing her daughter to marry the hero. In Klušin's *Smex i gore,* the maidservant

---

[34]  W. Lednicki, "Gribojedow a Polska", in his *Przyjaciele moskale* (Cracow, 1932), pp. 45-62.
[35]  Vl. Orlov, *op. cit.*, p. 4.
[36]  V. Asmus, "*Gore ot uma* kak estetičeskaja problema", *Lit. nasledstvo*, 47-8 (Moscow, 1946), pp. 193-6.

dresses up as the heroine, to give the latter time to wed the hero in a near-by church. Krylov based *Prokazniki* and *Urok dočkam* on the comic opportunities of situation provided by the "travestissement" popular in French comedy, and Knažnin employed the "double travestissement" in his comic opera *Mužja ženixi svoix žen* ("Husbands Affianced to their Spouses"), where master and valet, as well as mistress and maid disguise themselves.

The comedy of situation depended for much of its effect on the use of coincidence and accident in the development of the intrigue. Even Fonvizin was not averse to using these devices in *Nedorosl'*; Starodum's arrival at the Prostakov estate just in time to contribute to the development of the intrigue and the final denouement is as unexpected as the coincidence which brings the hero Milon to the neighbourhood where his sweetheart Sofia, whom he has seen for six months, happens to be staying. Fonvizin's concern for providing opportunities for moralising was clearly greater than his concern for originality of plot or plausibility in the use of accident and coincidence.

In the French theatre, the comedy of situation was developed by Beaumarchais to the point where pre-occupation with ingenuity of plot and construction overshadowed the portrayal of characters. His *Mariage de Figaro* was produced in St.-Petersburg in a Russian adaptation in 1787 and although the play was admired, the comedy of situation proper did not begin to flourish on the Russian stage until the 1810s. Moralising, satire and even "bytovoj" detail had no place in these comedies of situation, which were based on French models and centred upon a small group of persons, such as husband, wife, lover and lady's maid. The intrigue was concerned for the most part with an amusing misunderstanding or depicted a diverting oddity in human nature. A typical example was Griboedov's *Molodye suprugi* ("The Young Married Couple", 1815), freely adapted from Lesser's *Le Secret de Ménage*; this play, with its symmetrical and ingenious plot was orientated to the sophisticated audiences of the capital. So artificial were the plots of these comedies of situation that they were described as a "game of whist",[37] and were known in the French theatre as the "chassé croisé" device.

In the plays of Xmel'nickij, however, these plots reached a point beyond which the playwright's ingenuity could not go, and the genre contributed little to the development of the Russian theatre.

[37] Akademija nauk S.S.S.R., *Istorija russkoj literatury*, V (Leningrad, 1941), p. 304.

## IV

### *The Sentimental Comedy*

The mixed genre known in France as the "comédie larmoyante" or sentimental drama, originated in the English theatre with Lillo's *George Barnwell, or The London Merchant* (1731). This play, with its powerful moral lesson and bourgeois setting, was in many ways a reaction against the bawdry of Restoration comedy. It was produced in Paris in 1748 and reached St.-Petersburg in 1764. But the "effrayante moralité et sinistres tableaux" [38] of Lillo's play and of the still more successful *Gamester* by Moore (London 1753; Paris 1762; St.-Petersburg 1773) proved too powerful for the "singularly delicate and timid audiences" outside England. [39] The French playwrights, on whose versions the Russian adaptations were based, preferred to borrow the sentimental elements from these dramas and add them to their own comedies. The powerful prison and execution scenes in the English sentimental dramas were omitted in the French – and later Russian – versions, and writers such as Destouches, Nivelle de la Chaussée, Diderot and Mercier moved their audiences to admire virtue rather than to detest wickedness.

Diderot established the "comédie sèrieuse", which "has as its object the virtue and duties of man". [40] His *Le Fils naturel* (1757) and *Le Père de famille* (1760) "echoed the reformative and humanitarian temper of the age" [41] and were both translated into Russian in 1765, though they were not staged. Elagin translated nearly all the comedies of Destouches, to whom Lukin referred with admiration in the preface to his own sentimental comedy *Mot* (1765). Lukin declared that the influence of Destouches and Nivelle de la Chaussée on the taste of Russian audiences persuaded him to introduce "touching scenes" into this play. He incorporated "passages appropriate for arousing pity . . . though, as for the rest of the spectators, I tried to divert them by comic personages". [42]

Several of Mercier's popular "drames" were also performed in Rus-

---

[38] Felix Gaiffe, *op. cit.*, p. 54.

[39] *Ibid.*, p. 22.

[40] Denis Diderot, *Œuvres complètes*, VII (Paris, 1875), pp. 308-9.

[41] Denis Diderot, *Writings on the theatre*, ed. by F. C. Green (Cambridge, 1936), p. 8.

[42] Jules Patouillet, "La lettre de Voltaire à Sumarokov", *Revue de litt. comparée*, 7 (1927), p. 446.

sian, including *Ložnyj drug* ("The False Friend", 1779) and *Beglec* ("The Deserter", 1784). But by far the most successful of the French "comédies larmoyantes" to appear in a Russian version was Beaumarchais' *Eugènie*, produced in Moscow in 1770. Just before this production, Sumarokov declared his contempt for the "new and harmful species" of sentimental comedy-drama. He expressed this in the preface to his tragedy *Dmitrij Samosvanec* (1769), and in a letter to Voltaire which, however, has not survived.[43] But by this time Sumarokov's prestige was already in decline, and the public continued to frequent productions of sentimental comedy as well as the comedies of manners.

There was an essential difference between the sentimental comedy of Western Europe and the examples written by the Russian playwrights and adapters. Originally, sentimental comedy was written for middle-class audiences, and this bourgeois aspect was considered an essential element by practitioners of the genre. Russian sentimental comedy does not reflect this element. Audiences remained basically gentlefolk. So, despite the introduction by the Russian playwrights of merchants, petty officials, shop-keepers and the like into their comedies, there was little or no change in the constitution of the audiences. What changes there were took place in the content of the plays themselves.

A feature of the sentimental comedy which appealed to Russian writers was the way in which it alternated comic with affecting scenes. Lukin's exploitation of this method in his *Mot* led to the introduction into comedies and comic operas of "tearful scenes". Though often irrelevant to the plot and satirical purpose of the comedies, such scenes had the advantage of novelty and gave actors the opportunity to display their talents in dramatic scenes. Matinskij introduced into his comic opera *Sankpeterburskij gostinnyj dvor* (1781) an affecting scene in which a widow and her children implore the hard-hearted usurer Skvalygin to take pity on their plight: but the scene has nothing to do with the rest of the action, it tells the audience nothing they did not already know, and the widow with her children does not appear again after this single scene.

The impression created in the Russian theatre by the „comédie larmoyante" is evident in Fonvizin's *Nedorosl'*. Plavil'ščikov and (later) Vjazemskij both discerned "tearful" elements in the final scenes of

---

[43]  *Ibid.*, p. 449. The preface is reprinted pp. 451-4.

this play.[44] The concern of Starodum, the play's "raisonneur", with virtue and duty echoes Diderot's claim that "la vertu et les devoirs de l'homme" were particularly suitable themes for "comédie larmoyante". The final scene of *Nedorosl'*, in which Mrs. Prostakova is rejected by her ungrateful son, resembles a similarly affecting scene in Xeraskov's best-remembered sentimental drama *Nenavistnik* ("The Hater", 1779) in which a daughter turns against her father. The scene is also reminiscent of sentimental drama in its tableau arrangement: Mitrofan spurns his mother who swoons away, Sofia and Starodum hasten to her aid and Pravdin reproaches Mitrofan. As Mrs. Prostakova recovers her senses, Starodum "points at her" and brings the play to a close with the curtain-line "Behold the well-deserved fruits of evil conduct!"

Fonvizin's contemporaries found this denouement and accompanying tableau "particularly successful".[45] It was characteristic of writers of sentimental comedy that they often preferred to substitute a "tableau" for a "coup de théâtre". Moore's *Gamester* ends with a tableau in which Mrs. Beverley "falls at the feet of her spouse, who brings the children to the feet of their father and their mother to the other side, then gazes upon them all as he declares: 'Death, how I feel your terrors now!' He expires as Mrs. Beverley swoons away, and the curtain falls." [46]

Although comedy often borrowed effects and characters from sentimental comedy-dramas, the results of the importation of the genre into Russia was more apparent in classical tragedy, which the "comédie larmoyante" eventually ousted from the stage almost entirely. The process follows the general trend to be discerned in the development of all literary genres, where a higher literary kind is very often contaminated and then ousted by a lower kind. Comedy, being a low kind, was by its very nature less affected than the prestige-laden tragedy.

Sentimental drama, variously known as "sleznaja drama", "meščanskaja komedija" or "meščanskaja tragedija" became increasingly popular towards the end of the eighteenth century, with performances of Kotzebue's dramas, and the dramatised versions of sentimental novels by Il'in, Fedotov, and others. For a period, the theatres of St.-Peters-

---

[44]  K. V. Pigarev, *Tvorčestvo Fonvizina* (Moscow, 1954), pp. 189-200: R. E. Šames, ed., *Fonvizin v russkoj kritike* (Moscow, 1958), p. 10.
[45]  K. V. Pigarev, *op. cit.*, p. 189.
[46]  Quoted from the Polish translation of 1777, from J. Pawlowiczowa, *Drama mieszczanska* (Warsaw, 1955).

burg and Moscow staged sentimental comedies and dramas to the exclusion of everything else. But by this time, the genre had ceased to be comedy.

## V

### Comic Opera and Vaudeville

Comic opera as a genre was closely connected with satirical comedy, though its satire tended, naturally enough, to be milder in tone. However, comic opera libretti introduced many of the new, realistic and "bytovoj" social themes, characters and effects familiar in the comedy of manners.

Comic operas had been performed at the Imperial court in the 1740s, when Russian fairy-tale themes were adapted for the stage. The genre flourished most, however, after the success of Popov's *Anjuta* in 1772. The popularity of this work was largely due to the picturesque details of everyday peasant life, stylised for theatrical purposes. The music, songs and dances also pleased audiences greatly, and enterprising writers soon followed Popov's example. Between 1772 and 1800, some 70 comic operas were written by Russian playwrights.[47]

Soon, the picturesque elements overshadowed both the comedy and the opera. Nikolev introduced a "thunder-storm interlude" into his *Rozana i Ljubim* (1776), and Matinskij's *Sanktpeterburkij gostinnyj dvor* depicted betrothal ceremonies which, indeed, constitute most of the second act of this piece. His libretto included specifically Russian details, such as the bread and salt ceremony for welcoming guests (II, 5), and references to "black teeth" as a sign of beauty (II, 7). The importance attached to these Russian elements is demonstrated in Plavil'ščikov's *Mel'nik-sbitenščik soperniki* ("The Miller and the Sbiten-vendor as Rivals", 1782), produced shortly after the success of Knjažnin's *Sbitenščik* and Ablesimov's *Mel'nik-koldun*. The winner of the "rivalry" referred to in Plavil'ščikov's title is the Miller, because he is "all Russian", whereas no one knows where the Sbitenseller comes from – a veiled hint at the marked similarity audiences had

---

[47] V. V. Kallaš and N. E. Efros, *Istorija russkogo teatra*, I (Moscow, 1914), p. 131.

already discerned between Knjažnin's Stepan and Beaumarchais' Figaro.

Satire and moralising borrowed from the comedy of manners appear in such libretti as Knjažnin's *Nesčaste ot karety,* which derides Gallomania and its effect upon ignorant provincial gentry, and in Krylov's *Kofejnica,* satirising superstition among the same social class and deploring their inhumanity towards peasants.

However, most influence in the comic opera libretti was exerted by the sentimental comedy. Thus the purpose of Nikolev's *Rozana i Ljubim* was to show that "peasants have feelings".[48] Majkov's *Derevenskij prazdnik* ("A Rural Holiday", 1777) suggests its sentimental treatment of the landowner-serf relationship by the sub-title *Uvenčannaja dobrodetel'* ("Virtue Crowned"). Xeraskov, best known for his sentimental dramas, embarked into libretti with his *Dobrye soldaty* ("The Good Soldiers", 1779), which contains sentimental scenes and motifs.

The satirical element, never strong in comic opera libretti, began to disappear altogether in the mid-1780s, partly as a result of Catherine's dislike of the use of such themes. She attempted to counter them by writing comic opera libretti of her own, into which she introduced allegorical and fairy-tale subjects. By 1790, comic opera was overshadowed by comedy proper as a vehicle for satire, and was being transformed into the vaudeville, as exemplified by Gorčakov's *Kalif na čas* ("Caliph for an Hour") and *Baba-Jaga.* These, and numerous other pieces, consisted of little more than a slight plot made palatable with couplets and music,[49] and were often written as vehicles for popular actors and actresses to display their talents on benefit nights. Levšin entitled his *Mnimye vdovcy* ("The Supposed Widowers" 1794) a "komedija-vodevil" to indicate that it was neither a comedy nor a comic opera. As a minor genre, the vaudeville – a kind of operetta on national themes – flourished in the early nineteenth century, partly because Paul I was particularly fond of the species.[50] It has survived to the present.[51]

---

[48] P. N. Berkov, *Russkaja komedija* . . ., pp. 43-9.
[49] E. Legouve, quoted in *Papers on play-making,* ed. by Brander Mathews (New York, 1957), p. 262.
[50] R. A. Mooser, *op. cit.,* p. 179.
[51] V. V. Uspenskij, *Russkij vodevil'* (Leningrad, 1957), pp. 3-50.

## VI

### *The Unities*

Just as the distinctions between literary genres were respectfully observed by writers, readers and critics of the eighteenth century, so too the playwrights of the period regarded the unities and rules as rational and inspired truths, not merely traditional mechanical devices. The unities were believed to provide verisimilitude and render plays closer to "Nature" (as understood by contemporary theoreticians). The respect accorded to the unities by eighteenth-century playwrights derived from the notion that they had been formulated by Aristotle, though in fact the notion originated from eighteenth-century theoreticians such as Chapelain and Boileau. In any case, Aristotle's *Poetics* deals only with tragedy, and since comedy was a low genre, playwrights – including the Russians – allowed themselves a certain amount of freedom in interpreting the rules regarding unities of time, place and action. Sumarokov, for instance, appears not to have concerned himself with them at all.[52] On the whole, however, the Russian playwrights evidently agreed with Plavil'ščikov, who decided it was "absurd not to observe the unities".[53]

The unity of time appears to have been regarded as the most important of the three. It was more clearly defined and easier to satisfy than the other two, since it merely required the action of a play to take place within a stated length of time, which itself varied from three to 24 hours. All three- and five-act comedies of the eighteenth-century observe this rule, often with a good deal of ingenuity. No one, however, was able to rival Molière who had performed a triumph of classical art in making the duration of *Le Misanthrope* coincide with the length of time required for its presentation on the stage.

A particular advantage of the unity of time was that a playwright could draw the attention of his audience to the way it was being observed. This was achieved by the simple device of referring whenever possible to specific times of day or night at which events were supposed to be taking place on the stage. The frequency of such references in eighteenth-century plays can only be explained by the playwrights' anxiety to prove that the unity of time was being carefully observed.

[52]   A. A. Kaev, *Russkaja literatura*, 3rd ed., I (Moscow, 1958), p. 488.
[53]   N. I. Mordovčenko, *op. cit.*, II, p. 107.

Catherine was observing the rule when she made characters in *Vorčalkina* declare that "it is three o'clock" (I, 3) and "already four o'clock" (I, 6). Fonvizin ends *Brigadir* Act II "at dinner time", Act III concludes "at tea-time". *Nedorosl'* Act II ends "at dinner time", and Act III opens just after dinner has ended. Fonvizin has used the interval between the acts for dinner, and makes his personages draw the attention of the audience to the device he is using. Starodum arranges to leave Prostakov's house "at seven o'clock tomorrow morning" (IV, 8), and this specific time is again referred to in the following scene. The last act thus takes place immediately before seven o'clock next day, and this is emphasised by Pravdin's references to "yesterday".

Time references similar to these occur in a large number of comedies. Characters in Kop'ev's *Obraščennyj mizantrop* declare it is "seven o'clock" (II, 3), "midday" (II, 8) and mention the serving of vodka "before dinner" (III, 9). Kapnist observed the unity of time in *Jabeda*, and makes it clear to the audience that a night is supposed to pass between Acts III and IV. Kropotov's *Famuška* begins with a stage direction: "Five o'clock in the morning is heard striking, then an alarm-clock rings", and the next scene introduces visitors to see Count Čistoserdov. His valet tells the visitors that the count "went to bed last night at three o'clock", then declares "Now it is time for the count to get up". However, the entire chronology of *Fomuška* is confused: Fomuška's grandmother declares her husband took part in the battle of Chirigin (1676), though a marriage contract, read aloud in the final scene of the play, is dated 1780, and the play was first produced in 1785. The hero Ostromyslov declares he is aged 20, and was at the battle of Česte (1770). Kropotov's disregard for chronological plausibility suggests he was more concerned with demonstrating to the audience that his play was constructed in accordance with the rules for unity of time. Larger units of time, which the audience would not notice while the play was in progress, could safely be ignored.

Although Knjažnin's most ambitious comedies *Čudaki* and *Xvastun* do not contain specific references to time, his *Sbitenščik* takes place – as the stage directions show – between "dawn" at the opening of Act I and "dusk" when the play ends in Act III.

Respect for the unity of time persisted into the nineteenth century. Šaxovskoj observed it in *Urok koketkam*; the opening scene informs the audience that the time is early morning, as Xolmskij hesitates to visit his aunt and sister "so early, lest I waken them". The first act concludes with the heroine deciding to "go and take the waters", Act III opens "after dinner" and the time of the last act is carefully prepared for in Act IV, when Leleva confides in Ol'gin that "I always take a stroll at eleven o'clock" in the evening. Ol'gin keeps this rendezvous in Act V, scene 5, and the darkness in which he meets the coquette Leleva is unexpectedly dispersed by a display of fireworks.

Zagoskin was equally punctilious in making clear to his audiences that the unity of time was being observed. Act II of his *Komedija protiv komedii* takes place "in the afternoon", implying that Act I occurred that same morning, and Act III will be evening. The second act of his *Večernika učennyx* likewise takes place in the afternoon, for Vol'gin complains "It is already three o'clock" and he is ready for his dinner (II, 7). Act II of *Dobryj malyj* ends at two o'clock, when Ladov announces it is "lunch time", and in the same way "dinner time" is announced in *Bogatonov v stolice* to bring Act II to a close.

Unity of place was variously interpreted by the Russian playwrights. Sumarokov and Fonvizin were satisfied with setting their comedies in "a room". Later, the setting expands to the "house" of Knjažnin's *Xvastun,* then the garden will be included, as in Krylov's *Prokazniki* and the comedies of Šaxovskoj and Zagoskin. Kop'ev's notions regarding the unity of place in *Obraščennyj mizantrop* included the house of Gur Filatich, that of the Count, the Lebedjanskii market-place and, finally, a military camp. However, the characters make it abundantly clear that all these places are within walking distance of one another.

Kapnist made effective theatrical use of the rule in *Jabeda*: the audience is informed that the provincial court-house has just been burned down, and its proceedings will therefore be held in the house of the corrupt judge Krivosudov, where the preceding action has also taken place. Kapnist suggests that justice itself is in the power of Krivosudov. The device had been used before, with the same implication, in Verevkin's *Toč v toč* ("Exactly So", 1774).

Šaxovskoj was the first Russian playwright to move the entire action of a five-act play out of doors. To give plausibility to the comings and goings of a large number of characters, he set *Urok koketkam* in "a space between two little houses, with a trellis across the background, dividing this part from an alley leading to the Spa: a gate in the trellis". The season is summer, so that encounters between various characters in the open air seem very natural. Zagoskin also ventured out of doors for settings in *Komedija protiv komedii* (Act II) and *Bogatonov v derevne* (Act IV). By this time, the art of scene designing and construction had progressed far beyond the restricted "room" of the eighteenth-century theatre.

Unity of action was the most difficult dramatic rule to observe, because none of the theoreticians were able to agree on what the term meant. French dramatists were not at all enlightening on the subject.[54] Generally speaking, unity of action seems to have required that the principal action of the play be the consequence of all the secondary actions, so that the suppression of any of the secondary actions would render the principal action partly incomprehensible.[55] But it is often almost impossible to disentangle the principal from the secondary actions in Russian comedy, because the playwrights themselves set little store by the hierarchy. The love intrigue sometimes appears to form the main subject, though the ingenious plots practised by valets or chamber-maids occupy more time on the stage.

Griboedov's use of the three unities in *Gore ot uma* illustrates yet again his method of employing traditional formulae to suit his own dramatic purpose. The action takes place in Famusov's house in Moscow, but different parts of the house are shown, ranging from an antechamber to a hall with "a series of illuminated rooms" opening from it, and the "main entrance hall, with a large staircase from the second floor", and a doorkeeper's lodge to one side. The action takes place within a little over twelve hours, and references to specific times of day recur; however, instead of using these references merely to prove that the unity of time was being observed, Griboedov makes them essential components of the action.

In the first scene a diverting passage develops briefly as Sofia and Liza argue what o'clock it is, and Liza manipulates the clock – only to be discovered doing so by Famusov as the clock "chimes and plays". The advent of evening and night in Acts II and IV respectively provide the opportunity for stage effects. The denouement takes place in darkness as "the last lamp goes out" (IV, 10), and the stage is illuminated only by Liza's candle, which she drops in alarm (IV, 12). Famusov's call for more lights in the penultimate scene gives force to the implication that Sofia's love for Molčalin can no longer be concealed and will soon be known in society. On the other had there is some implausibility in the handling of time on a wider scale. Čackij declares he has been travelling 45 hours when he first calls on Sofia, yet he re-

---

[54]  F. Gaiffe, *op. cit.*, p. 446.
[55]  Jacques Scherer, *La Dramaturgie classique en France* (Paris, 1950), pp. 103-4.

appears at the evening party that evening; and Sofia herself claims she has stayed up all night with Molčalin, though she is to be hostess the following evening at Famusov's soirée.

Contemporary critics declared that *Gore ot uma* violated the unity of action because it contains a "double intrigue" – Čackij's love for Sofia and his "social drama".[56] But the success of the play shows that the audiences were no longer concerned with this theoretical principle. Griboedov had abandoned the unity of action because his theme was more important than a formula. Part of his contribution to the development of the Russian theatre was his ability to use or jettison rules which hampered his predecessors.

## VII

### *Acts and Scenes*

Other rules playwrights were expected to obey concerned the division into acts. Full-length, ambitious comedies such as *Brigadir, Nedorosl', Čudaki, Xvastun, Jabeda, Urok koketkam* were divided into five acts: slighter plays, such as *O Vremja!, Prokazniki, Komedija protiv komedii* contained three acts, while comic operas might contain only two. One acts plays were used either as "Nachkömedie" or as curtain-raisers to a longer play.

Division into acts, which was a traditional convention and is of obscure origin,[57] was perhaps necessary in the eighteenth century because the candles or oil-lamps used to illuminate the stage required attention every half-hour. The division of an act into scenes, also traditional, was strictly observed by all playwrights: a new scene began when a new character entered and introduced "new business".[58] The number of scenes that constituted an act was never defined, though Plavil'ščikov ironically suggested that a fixed number should be used.[59]

Although scene division may at first sight appear a purely mechanical arrangement, there is no doubt that the number of scenes in an act affected the tempo and pace of the play. Some of Krylov's comedies

---

[56] Vl. Orlov, "Xudožestvennaja problematika Griboedova", *Lit. nasledstvo*, 47-8 (Moscow, 1946), pp. 40-43.
[57] John Dryden, *Of dramatic poesy*, p. 33, note 4.
[58] *Ibid.*, p. 37.
[59] N. I. Mordovčenko, *op. cit.*, II, p. 107.

and libretti contain as many as 16 scenes to an act, suggesting that these plays were livelier and faster-moving on the stage than plays such as *Xvastun* or *Jabeda,* in which the number of scenes to an act rarely exceeds six or eight.

The end of each act was an important point in a play's structure. The playwright was required to furnish his characters with reasons for leaving the stage, as there were no curtains. Yet the audience's interest had to be maintained through the interval, which was therefore used for "time to be lost", when events not of sufficient interest to be depicted on the stage were supposed to take place. In classical French comedy, up to five such events might occur during the interval between act. Another difficulty confronting playwrights was that characters who appeared in the final scene of one act could not appear in the first scene of the succeeding act, as this implied that nothing had happened during the interval.[60] These "rules" were all observed in the Russian theatre, though with varying degrees of rigidity.

"Time to be lost" was often employed by eating and drinking off-stage. The interval between Acts II and III of *Nedorosl'* is occupied by the dinner to which Prostakova invites Pravdin; other dinners take place between Acts II and III of *Brigadir,* acts II and III of *Fomuška,* acts III and IV of *Obraščennyj mizantrop,* and acts III and IV of *Bogatonov.* Occasionally characters use the 'time to be lost" for drinking: the interval between acts IV and V of *Čudaki* is spent by Vysonos "drowning my sorrows in wine", and he reappears tipsy in act V. The court officials leave the stage in *Jabeda* to drink vodka (II, 6) and reappear in act III tipsy. Other examples of the use of "time to be lost" occur in *Obraščennyj mizantrop,* which is a particularly "well-made" play according to eighteenth-century standards: the interval between acts I and II is used for the delivery of a letter by the footman Dmitrij, who is seen leaving Gur Filatič' house in act I and who enters the count's house bearing the letter in act II, 1. Between acts II and III the count and Pravdin walk to the house of Gur Filatič, where they appear in act III, sc. 6. Between acts IV and V, the Count explains to his sister a number of facts already known to the audience, which would have been tedious if reported yet again on the stage.

Šaxovskoj used the formula in *Urok koketkam*; a group of charatcers no longer required on stage decide to "go for a walk", and are thus conveniently disposed of between acts III and IV, when they all

60   J. Scherer, *op. cit.,* pp. 208 ff.

return. That no time has been lost is indicated between acts III and IV of this play; the meeting arranged between Pronskij and Ol'gin in the final scene of act III is depicted in the first scene of act IV. The audience realised that no time had been lost in the interval because Pronskij appeared in both scenes. That the length of the "time to be lost" interval could be varied is illustrated by the interval of "two hours" supposed to elapse between acts IV and V of Zagoskin's *Bogatonov*.

## VIII

### Entrances and Exits

Entrances and exits were managed according to other formulae intended – like the other rules of classical theory – to add verisimilitude to plays. Thus playwrights were concerned to give their personages a reason for entering or leaving the stage. Corneille held this rule as "indispensable", adding: "there is nothing worse than an actor who leaves the stage merely because he has nothing more to say".[61]

One of the most frequent reasons for a character to enter was provided by the "search" formula, when a personage declares he or she is "looking for" someone. Almost all the eighteenth-century playwrights employed it; they included Fonvizin (*Ned.*, II, 5), Catherine (*O Vremja!*, I, 8), Krylov (*Soč.*, I, 1; II, 1; II, 9: *Prok.*, III, 3; IV, 6), Knjažnin (*Xvastun*, I, 3; IV, 2; *Čudaki*, II, 4; V, 7), Kapnist (*Jabeda*, I, 1) and Plavil'ščikov (*Bobyl'*, I, 2; II, 9). In addition to the "search" formula, the "inquiry" formula proved equally useful; here a character enters to inquire what is happening, often during a noisy brawl or quarrel. It is used by Fonvizin (*Brig.*, II, 2), Knjažnin (*Xvastun*, IV, 6; *Čudaki*, II, 2-3), Catherine (*O Vremja!*, III, 2; *Vorčalkina*, IV, 7), Kapnist (*Jabeda*, V, 8) and in comic opera (*SPD*, III, 3).

Despite Corneille's respect for the formula, however, it was regarded as artificial, and was rarely used more than two or three times in the same play.

The entry of a character was almost invariably announced by another character already on stage declaring "Here he (or she) is!" Often the name of the new character would be included. This device served two

---

[61]   Pierre Corneille, *Œuvres*, I (Paris, 1862), p. 108.

purposes; it was a cue to the actor about to enter, and it helped the audience identify him. Such announcements may occur as much as eight or even ten lines in advance of the character's entry, the delay being due to the structure of the stage itself. This was long and deep, so that a character entering from the rear would be perceived by the characters already on stage and by the audience as he or she advanced towards the footlights to take up their cue. The "here he is!" formula occurs in all the comedies of this period, up to and including those of Šaxovskoj and Zagoskin. Nevertheless, the artificiality of the device was sometimes ridiculed by the addition of remarks such as "Just in time!" or "Very apropos!", much as Molière unashamedly underlined such coincidences in *Le Misanthrope* (III, 4) and other plays.

Griboedov handled the problem of providing cues and identifying his characters in *Gore ot uma* in a more skilful and natural manner. Liza's cry "Ah, my master" greets Famuzov's entrance, and he in turn addresses Molčalin by name when the latter first appears (I, 4). Čackij's entrance, however, is announced by a footman, as in any well-conducted household, and later he is addressed by his first name and patronymic which the footman had already provided. Griboedov was able to avoid much of the awkward and implausible explanations required when a character entered or left the stage, because in *Gore ot uma* most of the characters are guests at Famusov's house. It was thus more natural for these persons to be addressed by their names when they appear.

Once a character has been identified, Griboedov abandoned the devices of his predecessors and expected his audience to follow the intrigue without being reminded, whenever a personage appears, of his or her rank, name and relationship to others.

The "flight" formula was convenient for arranging exits when a character had nothing more to say. Mitrofan flees from Vral'man, who in turn flees from Cyfirkin (*Ned.*, III, 8-9), and the device is also used in *Fomuška* (IV, 5), *Vorčalkina*, (I, 4) and elsewhere. When "flight" could not plausibly be used, playwrights invented other equally plausible reasons for their characters to quit the scene: "I have business to attend to . . ." "I must change my clothes . . ." "I must write a letter . . ." are all used in *Obraščennyj mizantrop* (II, 4, 6). Sometimes a character explains his exit by declaring he is going to greet new arrivals (*O Vremja!*, I, 10; *Obr. miz.*, V, 6; *Brig.*, II, 2), or to tell someone else what has just happened (*Vorč.*, IV, 12).

## IX

### *The Exposition*

Rules also existed for the exposition and denouement of plays. Ideally, the exposition should contain the "foundations of all the action, and close the way to anything one might want to introduce into the rest of the piece".[62] Boileau's view was that "the subject can never be introduced too soon".[63] The ideal exposition should also "present all the elements of the coming intrigue, and prepare the way for the first great peripetie". Furthermore, "no character should appear in later acts who has not been introduced during the exposition".[64]

However, these rules – like the rules governing the use of the three unities – were not always adhered to in the low genre of comedy. In many comedies, the first act was too large a space to fill with exposition, and even as skilful a playwright as Fonvizin was obliged to advance the entrance of the hero (of *Brigadir*) to the second scene of act I, although the traditional place for his appearance was act II. The intrigue of *Brigadir* is set in motion in the third scene of this act, by which time all the characters have been introduced and the first "great peripety" (the unexpected arrival of Dobroljubov) is disposed of in the first scene. The exposition of *Nedorosl'* occupies more space; the first peripety does not occur till scene 6, when Sofia announces the unexpected arrival of Starodum and his decision to make her his heiress. This peripety sets the intrigue in motion, and the arrival of the hero Milon is postponed to the more usual place (act II).

Fonvizin succeeded in casting the exposition of both these plays into the form of dialogue between most of the principal characters. In this respect, he was more skilful than his contemporaries, many of whom were content to use the archaic method of exposition as a monologue. Such monologues were often delivered by a minor personage, such as a servant. Examples of this method occur in *Fomuška,* where the valet Mitrofan soliloquises upon the Count's household for the information of the audience, in *Obraščennyj mizantrop* and in *Xvastun.* An equally archaic method was the expository dialogue, which is often a continuation of the expository monologue: the valet Dmitrij (*Obr. miz.*), having delivered his monologue, is joined by the heroine's maid, and

---

[62]  *Ibid.,* p. 43.
[63]  Boileau, *L'Art poétique,* III, p. 37.
[64]  Pierre Corneille, *Œuvres,* I (Paris, 1862), p. 43.

they both discuss the plight in which the heroine finds herself as the play opens. Other comedies which followed this pattern were Sumarokov's *Opekun*, Lukin's *Ščepetiľnik*, Catherine's *O Vremja!* and Knjažnin's *Čudaki*. Kapnist provided an expository dialogue of 200 lines – one of the longest in any comedy – to open *Jabeda*. Two decades later Šaxovskoj was still using the threadbare device in *Urok koketkam* and *Pustodomy*. It was left to Griboedov to find a variation on the device in *Gore ot uma*, which opens in the middle of a situation.

In addition to their expository function, monologues were copiously employed to provide continuity between scenes. The art of transition was highly regarded in the eighteenth century, and the skilful liaison of scenes was the mark of a "well-contrived" play.[65] This linking function enabled playwrights to observe yet another of the rules governing dramaturgy; this required that the stage never remain empty during the course of an act (this would mean that the act was finished), and that "very seldom should the stage remain without somebody speaking".[66]

These monologues, delivered by a character immediately after the exit of a second and before the appearance of a third, could be used to explain a character's motives or, more often, to arouse and maintain the interest of the audience. The accepted method of achieving this was for the monologue to consist of exclamations of surprise, dismay, consternation or uncertainty as to the outcome of the scene that had just finished. This was the main function of the monologue in Russian comedy during this period.

However, the monologue had been derided in seventeenth-century French dramaturgy, and its survival in comedy a hundred years later can only be explained by the lowness of the genre. Actors also favoured monologues, however, because they could hold the stage alone for a time. Voltaire complained: "Every comedian wishes to shine by means of a lengthy monologue".[67] But the general feeling of disapproval towards monologues may have caused Fonvizin to be remarkably sparing in his use of the device, particularly when compared with his contemporaries. *Brigadir* contains only one monologue, *Nedorosl'* two brief examples. Kapnist too employed only one monologue in *Jabeda*, a play written strictly according to the classical canons. But other playwrights

---

[65]  John Dryden, *op. cit.*, p. 29: Corneille, *op. cit.*, p. 101.
[66]  Lope da Vega, *The new art of writing plays* (New York, 1914), p. 32, and Boileau, *L'art poétique*, III, pp. 407-8, 412.
[67]  J. Scherer, *op. cit.*, pp. 256-7.

were less nice: *Fomuška* contains nine, including one 60 lines in length, *Prokazniki* ten, *Sočinitel' v prixožei* six, and *Xvastun* seven. But audiences were not very critical of the use of this and other obsolete theatrical devices, providing the comedy fulfilled its main purpose, and amused them.

# X

## *The dénouement and "mot à la fin"*

The denouement cut the thread of the intrigue by removing all obstacles to the hero's courtship of the heroine. In doing so, the fate of all the other characters was settled too. Like the exposition, an ideal denouement was brief, but – as Krylov complained – "many authors set the denouement at the beginning of their fifth act, and the remainder has to be filled in with more denouements, giving an account of all the subsidiary characters".[68] However, Krylov added than not even Molière had been able to avoid this fault, and the Russian writers of comedy followed the example of their great French model in this respect as in so many others.

We need not look for startling originality in the denouements of eighteenth-century comedy. A favourite method for obtaining a suitable climax was that provided by a change of heart: persons who had previously opposed the hero's courtship could be effected in a variety of ways. Malan'ja's father (*Fom.*) is so unnerved by her attempt to do away with herself, that he repents and allows her to marry Ostromyslov: the "raisonneur" Česton (*Bobyl'*) persuades Anjuta's father to change his mind and let her marry Matvej: the count induces Gur Filatič (*Obr. miz.*) to let Ljubov wed Pravdin. Other changes of mind or of heart often come about as a result of the "unmasking" of the heroine's foolish suitor, who had previously been supported by the parents of the heroine, as when Mrs. Lentjagina discovers that Vetromax is a penniless pretender (*Čudaki*). The foolish characters in Šaxovskoj's plays are exposed, and the exposure causes a change of heart in other characters; the frivolity of the coquette Leleva is revealed in the penultimate scene of *Urok koketkam*, and Bogatonov's foolishness is exposed, shaming him into allowing Liza to wed the hero of Zagoskin's *Bogatonov*.

To ensure that the moral lesson of their plays had been grasped by

---

[68]   I. A. Krylov, *Sočinenija v dvux tomax*, II (Moscow, 1956), p. 353.

the audiences, playwrights terminate comedies with the "mot à la fin" inherited partly from French comedy but also from the epilogues of Russian folk plays.[69] Generally delivered directly to the audience by the last character to leave the stage, the "mot à la fin" might be in the form of couplets (*Čudaki, Xvastun*) or an epigram (*Bobyl'*). It was also customary for the "mot" to contain a reference to the title of the play (*Jabeda, Pustodomy*): Saša, the lady's maid, informs the audience "there is no advantage to be had from coquetry' (*Urok kok.*), and at the end of *Kakadu*, she makes a pointed reference to the "umniki" who have been satirised in he play.

The "mot à la fin" which concludes *Gore ot uma* shows the device widening its scope. Famusov's cry of dismay: "My God! What will the Princess Marja Alekseevna say?" is not only more in character than the epigrams delivered by servants in eighteenth-century comedies, but it also sets the seal on Čackij's defeat at the hands of society. The age of didacticism in the Russian theatre was over.

---

[69]   B. V. Kuz'mina, *Russkij demokratičeskij teatr XVIII v.* (Moscow, 1958), p. 202.

# LIST OF WORKS CITED

Afanas'jev, A., *Russkie satiričeskie žurnaly* (Moscow, 1859).

Akademija nauk S.S.S.R., *Istorija russkoj literatury*, V (Leningrad, 1941).

Akademija nauk S.S.S.R., Institut filosofii, *N. I. Novikov i ego sovremenniki* (Moscow, 1961).

Akademija nauk S.S.S.R., Institut istorii, *Voprosy formovanija russkoj narodnosti* (Moscow-Leningrad, 1958).

Akademija nauk S.S.S.R., Institut russkoj literatury, *XVIII vek; sbornik statej*, 5 vols. (Moscow-Leningrad, 1935-62).

Akademija nauk S.S.S.R., Institut russkoj literatury, *Problemy russkogo prosveščenija v literature XVIII v.* (Moscow-Leningrad, 1961).

Akademija nauk S.S.S.R., Institut russkoj literatury, *Iz istorii russkix literaturnix otnosčenij XVIII. v.* (Moscow-Leningrad, 1959).

Arxangel'skij, A. S., "Dramaturgija Ekaterinskoj epoxi", in V. V. Kallaš and N. E. Efros, *Istorija russkogo teatra*, I (Moscow, 1914), pp. 211-316.

Aseev, B. N., *Russkij dramatičeskij teatr XVII.-XVIII. veka* (Moscow, 1958).

Asmus, V., "Gore ot uma kak èstetičeskaja problema", in *Literaturnoe nasledstvo*, 47-48 (1946), pp. 189-214.

d'Aubignac, *abbé* Francois, *Le pratique du théâtre*, ed. Pierre Martino (Paris, 1927).

B., V., "Vladimir Ignat'evič Lukin", *Ežegodnik imperatorskix teatrov*, IV, supp. 2 (1893-4), pp. 147-60.

Barskov, Ja. L., *Perepiska moskovskix masonov* (Petrograd, 1915).

Belinskij, V. G., "Obozrenie russkoj literatury ot Deržavina do Puškina", *Polnoe sobranie sočinenij*, VII (Moscow, 1953), pp. 99-131.

Berkov, P. N., *Aleksandr Petrovič Sumarokov 1717-1777* (Leningrad, 1949).

Berkov, P. N., "Dramatičeskij slovar' 1787 g.", in AN SSSR. Institut russkoj literatury, *Iz istorii russkix literaturnix otnošenij XVIII v.* (Moscow-Leningrad, 1959), pp. 52-65.

Berkov, P. N., *Russkaja komedija i komičeskaja opera XVIII v.* (Moscow-Leningrad, 1950).

Berkov, P. N., ed., *Satiričeskie žurnaly N. I. Novikova* (Moscow-Leningrad, 1951).

Blagoj, D. D., *Istorija russkoj literatury XVIII v.* (Moscow, 1960).

Borgerhoff, Elbert B. O. E., *Evolution of literary theory and practice in the French theatre 1680-1757* (Princeton, 1936).

Brodskij, N. L., *Literaturnye salony i kružki* (Moscow-Leningrad, 1930).

Bulič, N. N., *Sumarokov i sovremennaja emu kritika* (SPb., 1854).

Catherine II, *Sočinenija imperatricy Ekateriny II: proizvedenija literaturnye*, ed. A. I. Vvedenskij (SPb., 1893).

Corneille, Pierre, *Œuvres* (Paris, 1862).

Danilov, S. S., "K istoriografii russkogo dorevoljucionnogo i sovetskogo teatra I", in Leningradskij gos. teatral'nyj institut im. A. N. Ostrovskogo, *Zapiski o teatre* (1958), pp. 195-211.

Danilov, S. S., *Russkij dramatičeskij teatr XIX v.*, I (Leningrad, 1957).

Desnickij, V., "Social'no-političeskie i kul'turno-istoričeskie predposylki razvitija russkoj literatury v konce XVIII v.", in *Izbrannye stat'i po russkoj literature XVIII-XIX vv.* (Moscow-Leningrad, 1958), pp. 38-91.

Desterresnoires, G., *La comédie satirique au XVIIIe siècle* (Paris, 1885).

Diderot, Denis, *Writings on the theatre*, ed. by F. C. Green (Cambridge, 1936).

Diderot, Denis, *Œuvres complètes* (Paris, 1875).

Dobroljubov, N. A., "Russkaja satira v veke Ekateriny II", in his *Sobranie sočinenija v 3-x tomax*, II (Moscow, 1952), pp. 316-400.

Dryden, John, *Of dramatic poesy*, ed. by George Watson (London, 1962).

Elizarova, N. A., *Teatry Šeremetovyx* (Moscow, 1944).

Evrejnov, N. N., *Istorija russkogo teatra s drevnejšix vremen do 1917 goda* (New York, 1955).

Fonvizin, D. I., *Sočinenija, pis'ma i izbrannye perevody D. I. Fonvizina*, ed. by P. A. Efremov (SPb. 1866).

Fournel, F. V., *Le théâtre au XVIIe siècle; la comédie* (Paris, 1892).

Frederick, Edna C., *The plot and its construction in 18th-century French criticism of French comedy* (Bryn Mawr, 1934).

Gaiffe, Felix, *Le drame en France au XVIIIe siècle* (Paris, 1910).

Geršenson, M., *Griboedovskaja Moskva*, 2d ed. (Moscow, 1916).

Gogol', N. V., "V čem že nakonec suščestvo russkoj poezii i v čem eje osobennost'?", in his *Polnoe sobranie sočinenija*, VIII (Leningrad, 1952), pp. 369-408.

Gooch, G. P., *Catherine the Great, and other studies* (London, 1954).

Gordin, A. M., ed., *A. S. Griboedov v russkoj kritike* (Moscow, 1958).

Gorodeckij, E. P. and others, *Istorija russkoj kritiki*, I (Moscow-Leningrad, 1958).

Green, F. C., *Minuet* (London, 1935).

Griboedov, A. S., *Sočinenija*, ed. Vl. Orlov (Moscow, 1953).

Griboedov, A. S., *Gore ot uma*, ed. D. Costello (Oxford, 1951).

Gukovskij, G. A., *Očerki po istorii russkoj literatury i obščestvennoj mysli XVIII v.* (Leningrad, 1938).

Gukovskij, G. A., *Xrestomatija po russkoj literature XVIII v.*, 3rd ed. (Moscow, 1938).

Gukovskij, G. A., *Russkaja literatura XVIII v.* (Moscow, 1939).

Gurevič, L. Ja., *Istorija russkogo teatral'nogo byta*, I (Moscow, 1934).

Hankiss, J., *P.-N. Destouches* (Debrecen, 1918).

Haumant, E., *La culture française en Russie*, 2nd ed. (Paris, 1913).

Hubert, J. D., *Molière and the comedy of intellect* (Stanford, 1962).

Ivanov, I., *Političeskaja rol' francuzskogo teatra v svjazi s filosofiei XVIII-ogo v.* (Moscow, 1895).

Ivanov-Razumnik, V., *Istorija russkoj obščestvennoj mysli*, I, 2nd ed. (SPb., 1908).

Kaev, A. A., *Russkaja literatura*, 3rd ed. (Moscow, 1958).

Kallaš, V. V. and N. E. Efros, eds., *Istorija russkogo teatra*, I (Moscow, 1914).

Kapnist, V. V., *Sobranie sočinenij*, ed. D. S. Babkin, 2 vols. (Moscow-Leningrad, 1960).

Klabunovskij, I. G. and A. Slonimskij, *A. S. Griboedov: sbornik statej* (Moscow, 1946).

Klejber, Boris, "Zagadki *Gorja ot uma*", *Scando-Slavica*, VIII (1961), pp. 20-44.

Ključevskij, V. O., *Kurs russkoj istorii*, Pt. 5 (Moscow, 1937).

Knjažnin, Ja. V., *Sobranie sočinenij*, 2 vols. (SPb., 1848).

Knjažnin, Ja. V., *Izbrannye proizvedenija*, ed. by L. I. Kulakova (Leningrad, 1961).

Kokorev, A. V., ed., *Xrestomatija po russkoj literature XVIII v.*, 3rd ed. (Moscow, 1961).

Krjažimskaja, I. A., "Iz istorii russkoj teatral'noj kritiki konca XVIII – načala XIX v.", in AN SSSR. *XVIII v.*, IV (1959), pp. 106-229.

Krjažimskaja, I. A., "Teatral'no-kritičeskie stat'i N. M. Karamzina", in AN SSSR. *XVIII v.*, III (1958), pp. 262-275.

Kruglyj, A. O., "I. P. Elagin. Biografičeskij očerk", in *Ežegodnik imp. teatrov*, IV, supp. 2 (1893-4), pp. 96-118.

Krylov, I. A., *Polnoe sobranie sočinenij*, ed. by V. V. Kallaš, 4 vols. (SPb., 1904).

Krylov, I. A., *Sočinenija v dvux tomax* (Moscow, 1956).

Kuz'mina, B. V., *Russkij demokratičeskij teatr XVIII v.* (Moscow, 1958).

Lang, D. M., "Boileau and Sumarokov; the manifesto of Russian classicism", *Mod. Lang. Review*, 43 (1958), pp. 500-506.

Lanson, G., *Nivelle de la Chaussée*, 2nd ed. (Paris, 1903).

Larivière, Charles de, *Cathérine II et la Révolution Française* (Paris, 1895).

Lednicki, W., "Gribojedow a Polska", in his *Przyjaciele moskale* (Cracow, 1932), pp. 45-62.

Leger, Louis, *La Russie intellectuelle; études et portraits* (Paris, 1914).

Lemaitre, J., *La comédie après Molière*, 2nd ed. (Leipzig, 1903).

Levrault, Leon, *La comédie – évolution du genre*, 11th ed. (Paris, 1900).

Linthilac, B., *Histoire générale du théâtre en France*, IV (Paris, n.d.).

Loftis, J. C., *Comedy and society: Congreve to Fielding* (Stanford, 1959).

Lo Gatto, Ettore, *Storia del teatro russo*, 2 vols. (Florence, 1952).

Longinov, M. N., *Novikov i moskovskie Martinisty* (Moscow, 1867).

Maclean, Hugh, "The development of modern Russian literature", *Slavic review*, 21 (1962), pp. 389-410.

Majkov, V. I., *Sočinenija i perevody* (SPb., 1867).

Makogonenko, G. N., *D. Fonvizin – tvorčeskij put'* (Moscow-Leningrad, 1961).

Makogonenko, G., *Nikolaj Novikov i russkoe prosveščenie XVIII v.* (Moscow-Leningrad, 1957).

Makogonenko, G., ed., *Russkaja dramaturgija XVIII v.*, I (Moscow-Leningrad, 1959) (vol. 2 edited by B. S. Mejlax).

Malnick, Bertha, "A. A. Šaxovskoj", *Slavonic and East European Review*, 32 (1953-4), pp. 28-51.

Malnick, Bertha, Review article of P. N. Berkov's *Russkaja komedija i komičeskaja opera XVIII v.*, in *Slavonic and East European Review*, 31 (1952-3), pp. 574-578.

Malnick, Bertha, "The theory and practice of Russian drama in the early 19th century", *Slavonic and East European Review*, 34 (1955-6), pp. 10-33.

Masson, C. F. P., *Mémoirs secrets sur la Russie*, 4 vols. (Paris, 1804).

Mathewson, R. W., "Russian literature and the West", *Slavic Review*, 21 (1962), pp. 411-417.

Matthews, Brander, ed., *Papers on play-making* (New York, 1957).

McKee, K. N., *The theater of Marivaux* (New York, 1958).

Mejlax, B. S., ed., *Russkie dramaturgi XVIII-XIX vv.*, II (Leningrad, 1961).

Mejlax, B. S., ed., *Russkie pisateli o literaturnom trude*, I (Moscow, 1954).

Meyer, M. M., *La convention dans le théâtre d'amour de Marivaux* (Sao Paulo, 1961).

Miles, Dudley H., *The influence of Molière on Restoration comedy* (New York, 1910).

Mooser, R. A., *L'Opéra-comique français en Russie au XVIIIe siècle* (Monaco-Geneva, 1954).

Mordovčenko, N. I., *Russkaja kritika pervoj četverti XIX v.* (Moscow, 1959).

Nečkina, M., *Griboedov i Dekabristy*, 2nd ed. (Moscow, 1951).

Noyes, G. R., *Masterpieces of the Russian drama* (New York, 1933).

Orlov, Vl., "Xudožestvennaja problematika Griboedova", *Lit. nasledstvo*, 47-48 (1946), pp. 3-76.

Palmer, John, *The comedy of manners* (London, 1913), reprinted New York, 1962.

Patouillet, Jules, "L'histoire du théâtre russe: essaie de bibliographie critique", *Revue des études slaves*, 2 (1922), pp. 125-46.

Patouillet, Jules, "La lettre de Voltaire à Soumarokov", *Revue de litt. comparée*, VII (1927), pp. 438-458.

Patouillet, Jules, "Molière et sa fortune en Russie", *Revue des études slaves*, 2 (1922), pp. 272-302.

Patouillet, Jules, *Le théâtre de mœurs russes* (Paris, 1912).

Pawlowiczowa, J., *Drama mieszczanska* (Warsaw, 1955).

Pigarev, K. V., *Tvorčestvo Fonvizina* (Moscow, 1954).

Pokrovskij, V. I., ed., *Fonvizin; žizn' i sočinenija* (SPb., 1903).

Pokrovskij, V. I., ed., *Griboedov: ego žizn' i sočinenija*, 3rd ed. (Moscow, 1911).

Pokrovskij, V. I., *N. I. Novikov; ego žizn' i sočinenija* (Moscow, 1910).

Pokrovskij, V. I., *Sumarokov: žizn' i sočinenija*, 2nd. ed. (Moscow, 1911).

*Puškin v teatre* (Moscow, 1953).

Pypin, A. N., *Istorija russkoj literatury*, IV (SPb., 1907).

Quénet, Charles, *P. I. Tchaadaev et les Lettres philosophiques* (Paris, 1931).

Raeff, M., "Home, school and service in the life of the eighteenth-century Russian nobleman", *Slavonic and East European Review*, 40 (1962), pp. 295-307.

Reeve, F. D., ed., *An anthology of Russian plays*, Vol. 1: *1790-1890* (New York, 1961).

Rogger, Hans, *National consciousness in eighteenth-century Russia* (Cambridge, Mass., 1960).

Rogger, Hans, "The Russian national character; some eighteenth-century views", *Harvard Slavic Studies*, IV 1957), pp. 17-34.

Rulin, P., "Elementy zlobodnevnosti v komedijax A. P. Sumarokova", *Slavia*, IV (1925-6), pp. 720-738.

Scherer, Jacques, *La dramaturgie classique en France 1630-1674* (Paris, 1950).

Selivanov, N. A., "Teatr v carstvovanie imperatricy Ekateriny II 1761-1796", *Ežegodnik imp. teatrov VI, supp. 2* (1895-6), pp. 15-76, and *supp. 3* (1895-6), pp. 86-117.

Semennikov, V. P., *Knigoizdatel'skaja dejatel'nost' N. I. Novikova* (Petersburg, 1921).

Serman, I. Z., "Komedija F. Emina: *Učenaja šajka*", AN SSSR. *XVIII v.*, III (1958), pp. 211-216.

Šames, R. E., ed., *Fonvizin v russkoj kritike* (Moscow, 1958).

Šamraj, D. D., "K istorii cenzurnogo režima Ekateriny II", AN SSSR. *XVIII v.*, III (1958), pp. 187-203.

Šaxovskoj, A. A., *Komedii: stixotvorenija*, ed. A. A. Gozenpud (Leningrad, 1961).

Sivkov, K. V., "Častnye pansiony i školy Moskvy v 80-ax godax XVIII veka", *Istoričeskij arxiv*, 6 (1951), pp. 315-323.

Skabičevskij, A. M., *Očerki istorij russkoj cenzury* (SPb., 1892).

Stepanov, N. L., *I. A. Krylov* (Moscow, 1958).

Štrange, M. M., *Russkoe obščestvo i francuzskaja revoljucija* (Moscow, 1956).

Sumarokov, A. P., *Polnoe sobranie vsex sočinenij* ... edited by N. Novikov, vols. V and VI (Moscow, 1781).

Tupikov, I. M., "Satira na Ablesimova", *Ežegodnik imp. teatrov*, IV, supp. 2 (1893-4), pp. 141-146.

Uspenskij, V. V., ed., *Russkij vodevil'* (Leningrad, 1959).

Varneke, B. V., *Istorija russkogo teatra XVII-XIV vv.*, 3rd ed. (Mocsow-Leningrad, 1939) (English translation New York, 1951).

Varneke, B. V., "Teatr pri Ekaterine II", in V. V. Kallaš and N. E. Efros, eds., *Istorija russkogo teatra*, I (Moscow, 1914), pp. 155-210.

Veselovksij, A., *Zapadnoe vlijanie v novoj russkoj literature*, 2nd ed. (Moscow, 1896).

Vinogradov, V. V., *Očerki po istorii russkogo literaturnogo jazyka* (Leiden, 1950).

Vjazemskij, P. A., *Polnoe sobranie sočinenij*, ed. by S. D. Šeremetev, V (SPb., 1880) (contains his *Fon-Vizin* of 1848).

Vsevolodskij-Gerngross, V., *Istorija russkogo teatra*, ed. by A. V. Lunačarskij, 2 vols. (Leningrad, 1929).

Vsevolodskij-Gerngross, V. N., *Kratkij kurs istorii russkogo teatra* (Moscow-Leningrad, 1936).

Vsevolodskij-Gerngross, V. N., *Russkij teatr vtoroj poloviny XVIII veka* (Moscow, 1960).

Wade Ira, O., *The "Philosophe" in the French drama of the 18th century* (Princeton, 1926).

Zagoskin, M., *Polnoe sobranie sočinenij*, 3 vols. (Moscow, 1904).

Žixarev, S. P., *Zapiski sovremennika* (Moscow-Leningrad, 1955).

# INDEX

# SLAVISTIC PRINTINGS AND REPRINTINGS

*Edited by C. H. van Schooneveld*

21. American Contributions to the Fourth International Congress of Slavicists, Moscow, September 1958. 1958. 427 pp. Cloth. Glds. 40.—
22. NIKOLAI DURNOVO: Očerk istorii russkogo jazyka. Photomechanic reprint. Second printing. 1962. 384 pp. Cloth. Glds. 24.—
23. PETER K. CHRISTOFF: An Introduction to Nineteenth-Century Russian Slavophilism. Volume I: A. S. Xomjakov. 1961. 301 pp., 2 plates. Cloth. Glds. 33.—
24. JOVAN BRKIĆ: Moral Concepts in Traditional Serbian Epic Poetry. 1961. 177 pp. Cloth. Glds. 24.—
25. JOSIP VRANA: L'Evangéliaire de Miroslav. Contribution à l'étude de son origine. 1961. 211 pp., 10 plates. Cloth. Glds. 48.—
27. Studies in Russian and Polish Literature. In Honor of Wacław Lednicki. Edited by Z. Folejewski, †M. Karpovich, F. J. Whitfield, A. Kaspin. 1962. 250 pp., portrait. Cloth. Glds. 36.—
28. WACŁAW LEDNICKI: Henryk Sienkiewicz. A Retrospective Synthesis. 1960. 81 pp., 7 plates. Glds. 15.—
29. A. M. VAN DER ENG-LIEDMEIER: Soviet Literary Characters. An Investigation into the Portrayal of Soviet Men in Russian Prose, 1917-1953. 1959. 176 pp. Cloth. Glds. 16.—
30. HENRY KUČERA: The Phonology of Czech. 1961. 112 pp. Cloth. Glds. 18.—
31. Taras Ševčenko, 1814-1861. A Symposium. Edited by Volodymyr Mijakovs'kyj and George Y. Shevelov. 1962. 302 pp. Cloth. Glds. 32.—
32. MICHAEL SAMILOV: The Phoneme jat' in Slavic. 1964. 172 pp. Cloth. Glds. 28.—
33. ROBIN KEMBALL: Alexander Blok. A Study in Rhythm and Metre. 1965. 539 pp., portrait. Cloth. Glds. 80.—
34. V. ŽIRMUNSKII: Voprosy teorii literatury. Statej 1916-1926. Photomechanic reprint. 1962. 356 pp. Cloth. Glds. 28.—
35. CHARLES E. PASSAGE: The Russian Hoffmannists. 1963. 261 pp. Cloth. Glds. 30.—
36. VSEVOLOD SETCHKAREV: Studies in the Life and Works of Innokentij Annenskij. 1963. 270 pp. Cloth. Glds. 32.—
37. A. I. SOBOLEVSKII: Lekcii po istorii russkogo jazyka. Photomechanic reprint. 1962. 308 pp. Cloth. Glds. 26.—
38. GEORGE Y. SHEVELOV: The Syntax of Modern Literary Ukrainian. The Simple Sentence. 1963. 319 pp. Cloth. Glds. 48.—
39. ALEXANDER M. SCHENKER: Polish Declension. A Descriptive Analysis. 1964. 105 pp., 38 figs. Cloth. Glds. 17.—
40. MILADA SOUČKOVA: The Parnassian Jaroslav Vrchlický. 1964. 151 pp., plate. Cloth. Glds. 20.—
41. A. A. ŠAXMATOV: Sintaksis russkogo jazyka. Redakcija i kommentarii Prof. E. S. Istrinoj. Photomechanic reprint. 1963. 623 pp. Cloth. Glds. 48.—
42. CHARLES A. MOSER: Antinihilism in the Russian Novel of the 1860's. 1964. 215 pp. Cloth. Glds. 22.—

MOUTON & CO · PUBLISHERS · THE HAGUE